AMAZON
Income:

How ANYONE of Any Age, Location, and/or Background Can Build a Highly Profitable Online Business with Amazon

By Sharon L. Cohen

Amazon Income: How ANYONE of Any Age, Location, and/or Background Can Build a Highly Profitable Online Business with Amazon

Copyright © 2010 Atlantic Publishing Group, Inc.
1405 SW 6th Avenue • Ocala, Florida 34471 • Phone 800-814-1132 • Fax 352-622-1875
Web site: www.atlantic-pub.com • E-mail: sales@atlantic-pub.com
SAN Number: 268-1250

Library of Congress Cataloging-in-Publication Data

Cohen, Sharon, 1949-
 Amazon income : how anyone of any age, location, and/or background can build a highly profitable online business with Amazon / by Sharon L. Cohen.
    p. cm.
Includes bibliographical references and index.
ISBN-13: 978-1-60138-299-3 (alk. paper)
ISBN-10: 1-60138-299-5 (alk. paper)
1. Amazon.com (Firm) 2. Electronic commerce. 3. Selling. I. Title.
HF5548.32.C63 2009
658.8'72--dc22
                                        2009009592

Printed in the United States

PROJECT MANAGER: Melissa Peterson • mpeterson@atlantic-pub.com
INTERIOR DESIGN: Holly Marie Gibbs • hgibbs@atlantic-pub.com
INTERIOR LAYOUT: Nick Wakerley • nick@thewrongcrowd.co.nz
ASSISTANT EDITOR: Angela Pham • apham@atlantic-pub.com

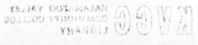

We recently lost our beloved pet "Bear," who was not only our best and dearest friend but also the "Vice President of Sunshine" here at Atlantic Publishing. He did not receive a salary but worked tirelessly 24 hours a day to please his parents. Bear was a rescue dog that turned around and showered myself, my wife, Sherri, his grandparents Jean, Bob, and Nancy, and every person and animal he met (maybe not rabbits) with friendship and love. He made a lot of people smile every day.

We wanted you to know that a portion of the profits of this book will be donated to The Humane Society of the United States. *–Douglas & Sherri Brown*

The human-animal bond is as old as human history. We cherish our animal companions for their unconditional affection and acceptance. We feel a thrill when we glimpse wild creatures in their natural habitat or in our own backyard.

Unfortunately, the human-animal bond has at times been weakened. Humans have exploited some animal species to the point of extinction.

The Humane Society of the United States makes a difference in the lives of animals here at home and worldwide. The HSUS is dedicated to creating a world where our relationship with animals is guided by compassion. We seek a truly humane society in which animals are respected for their intrinsic value, and where the human-animal bond is strong.

Want to help animals? We have plenty of suggestions. Adopt a pet from a local shelter, join The Humane Society and be a part of our work to help companion animals and wildlife. You will be funding our educational, legislative, investigative and outreach projects in the U.S. and across the globe.

Or perhaps you'd like to make a memorial donation in honor of a pet, friend or relative? You can through our Kindred Spirits program. And if you'd like to contribute in a more structured way, our Planned Giving Office has suggestions about estate planning, annuities, and even gifts of stock that avoid capital gains taxes.

Maybe you have land that you would like to preserve as a lasting habitat for wildlife. Our Wildlife Land Trust can help you. Perhaps the land you want to share is a backyard—that's enough. Our Urban Wildlife Sanctuary Program will show you how to create a habitat for your wild neighbors.

So you see, it's easy to help animals. And The HSUS is here to help.

THE HUMANE SOCIETY
OF THE UNITED STATES

2100 L Street NW • Washington, DC 20037 • 202-452-1100
www.hsus.org

DEDICATION

To my amazing men, Jean, Seth, and Jordan.

Acknowledgements:

Thank you to the spirited e-entrepreneurs, who are included in this book, for their insights, information, and inspiration, and to Melissa Peterson of Atlantic Publishing for her support and patience.

TRADEMARK DISCLAIMER

# TABLE OF CONTENTS

Chapter 4: What is the Best Product to Sell?   53

Chapter 5: Selling in the Amazon Marketplace   65

Chapter 6: Start an Online Book Business with Amazon   83

Chapter 7: Using Amazon Marketplace to Sell Used Books   101

Chapter 24: Building Ties with the Online Community   295

Conclusion: Continuous Change at Amazon   309

Glossary   319

Bibliography   329

Author Biography   331

Index   333

 **FOREWORD**

Do you remember where you were when you heard wonderful, life-changing news? It was maybe 1996 or so that *The Wall Street Journal®* article that presented the news to me came out. I remember where I was — living in a temporary apartment just before the big move into a fabulous hilltop villa overlooking the San Fernando Valley in California. The front page article told about this little company with a funny name. People were buying books like crazy from them; they were growing like a weed. I studied every word of that article. This was something I had to look into because I had been marketing on the Internet since 1994, and this article described some magic called Amazon.com®. Over the next few years, Amazon® would take an inordinate role in my life. I visited them for the first time around 1999. What a funky company: One side of their building was a hospital. Across the hall was reception, and employees' dogs wandered the corridors. They even sold doggy treats at the in-house espresso bar.

The founder, Jeff Bezos, worked from a desk made from an old door placed on sawhorses. Everything was inexpensive, informal, and funky.

But Amazon was not a flippant dot-com here today and gone tomorrow. The people I visited were serious, and the smartest of the smart. They asked penetrating questions of my startup and were cautious as well as astute.

We did our deal, one of several, and by then, I had already bought thousands of dollars worth of books from them. Then, it was cookware, accessories, and electronics. I followed Amazon as they went into the auction business, the used-book business, and the fulfillment business.

Years later, the scene has changed. I still buy books and electronics from Amazon, but I do so much more.

For years, I struggled with the simple task of selling merchandise and having someone reliable ship it for me. Amazon fills that role now. They are masters of getting the goods out the door in a matter of hours. They rush whatever my customers order and never lose a thing. This is no small matter, and not many companies are masters of this the way Amazon is — maybe nobody on Earth fulfills better than they do. So, they do all my fulfillment for the products I sell.

They have always run an amazingly reliable and scalable server farm. They have to serve millions of customers at the height of the holiday rush hour, and seldom does their site even slow down.

So now, I use their servers — their S3^{SM} service — to serve videos and audios to the crowds that visit my sites, such as **www.Mort-gageRelief-Formula.com**. This S3 can show a million people the same video at the same time. You do not need to burden your own servers with this, and it costs peanuts compared to having your own computers set up to do the same thing.

Amazon's cleverness extends to other areas, and I use many of them. My programmers in one of my businesses are just now setting up a system that uses their database to store data and deliver it on-demand to my customers.

How many thousands of businesses has Amazon spawned that would not be providing a good living for entrepreneurs if Amazon had never existed? One startup I know built their entire business by selling on Amazon, and now, author Sharon L. Cohen, with her book *Amazon Income: How ANYONE of Any Age, Location, and/or Background Can Build a Highly Profitable Online Business with Amazon*, has turned me on to many other startups and business owners who are depending on Amazon and using Amazon to build their business in ways I never dreamed.

The press knows that eBay® has an interesting story here or there, such as an auction for babies, or the sale of a country (just kidding). But the real action often takes place away from the public eye. That is the case with Amazon. Cohen has revealed a most amazing story, a story of thousands of entrepreneurs quietly using Amazon to make money; a story that is still young and still affords a ground floor opportunity for the rest of us. We can take a good idea and, with Amazon's help, turn it into money. I love the thorough overview of the business possibilities and the case studies that Cohen shows us, and I think you will find it a thrilling ride with numerous opportunities for you. Thank you, Sharon, for writing this book.

Richard Geller, CEO
DesiredResultsPublishing, LLC
Fairfax, Virginia

 # INTRODUCTION

The Amazon Business Model of Change

For the foreseeable future, Amazon's business model will be included in academic textbooks as an example of an innovative e-business that braved the ups and downs of the Internet and continued to grow, adapt, and diversify its services. When Amazon opened its online store in July 1995, it defied all those who said it would never succeed. Its mission was to completely transform the book-buying concept by using online technology to enhance customer service, ease, and speed. The company soon expanded by adding many other products, such as movies, music, computer software, video games, electronics, clothing, toys, and even diamond rings. "Change" is the catchword for the Internet, and Amazon has followed this direction since its beginning. The business has regularly revamped its opportunities — trying out new ventures and expanding successful ones.

Many of the opportunities in this book were added or revised this past year. As with many Web ventures, men and women of all ages, backgrounds, experience levels, and geography have the ability with Amazon to open, develop, and grow a business right from their home office. As the information and case studies in this book demonstrate, Amazon offers a variety of opportunities, from incremental and long-tail money sources to main income generators, based on an individual's personal goals and level of participation and commitment. The customer is a No. 1 priority for Amazon, and so are its business partners.

Jeff Bezos and Customer-Centrism

By now, the story of Amazon founder Jeff Bezos, as described on **www.Amazon.com**, is quite well-known. In 1994, he was quickly climbing the top rings of the ladder as the youngest senior vice president in the history of D. E. Shaw, a Wall Street–based investment bank. He heard about a new record-breaking medium called the Internet, which was expanding at a remarkable 2,300 percent a year, and left Wall Street behind. Bezos decided to target books on this new Web platform, which was not the norm at that time. He relocated to Seattle, Washington, near the largest wholesalers, and began working out of his garage. His vision contained two main points. The first goal was to construct the largest and most customer-centric venture. The second goal was to establish an on-line location where customers could buy anything they wanted. As noted in a report in *Journal of Advertising Research*, he summed up this vision of customer-centrism as:

"Our goal is to be Earth's most customer-centric company. I will leave it to them to say if we've achieved that. But why? The answer is three things. The first is that customer-centric means figuring out what your customers want by asking them,

then figuring out how to give it to them, and then giving it to them. That's the traditional meaning of customer-centric, and we're focused on it. The second is innovating on behalf of customers, figuring out what they don't know they want and giving it to them. The third meaning, unique to the Internet, is the idea of personalization: Redecorating the store for each and every individual customer."

Many thought that Bezos was way off the mark when saying he wanted to give customers the opportunity to shop for millions of books. He quickly proved them wrong. Within its first month of business, Amazon filled orders for customers in 50 states and 45 countries — all shipped out of his garage. In 1996, its first full fiscal year, Amazon produced $15.7 million in sales. This number jumped by 800 percent the following year. However, selling books was just the foundation. His customer-centered innovations made the business all the more unique. These included many of the services now taken for granted, such as shopping carts, personalized shopping, and 1-click® shopping.

At this time, Amazon also pioneered affiliate marketing, with hundreds of thousands of sites linking to Amazon, including Yahoo!, AOL®, and MSN™. Amazon became the first Internet retailer to operate an affiliate program that allowed owners of other Web sites to refer customers to Amazon in return for a referral fee. To protect its unique proprietary technology, Amazon received a patent for a "1-click" shipping procedure and contributed to 600,000 affiliates by the first quarter of 2001. Since then, Amazon has teamed with its affiliates to expand its market reach well beyond its own domain and focus its strength on order fulfillment and distribution.

In 1997, the *Economist* declared, "Companies around the world are studying it [Amazon.com] as perhaps the best model for tomorrow's successes in electronic commerce." *The Wall Street Journal*® ranked the e-business among the top five firms "shaping the new age." In a nationwide survey of nearly 11,000 people conducted online by Harris Interactive Inc. and the Reputation Institute, Amazon was named among the top 25 best-regarded and most-visible U.S. companies in 1999 and 2000.

The Ups and Downs of the Internet Business

Amazon's first decade soared and spiraled downward like a rollercoaster. By the end of 1999, annual sales had grown to $1.6 billion. In December, *Time* magazine named Bezos "Person of the Year," calling him the "King of Cybercommerce." Yet, only a short month later, this same celebrated person had to dismiss 150 employees, mostly at the Seattle headquarters, as part of an internal reorganization. Then, just five days later, Amazon reported a loss of $323 million for the fourth quarter and promised that future losses would be lower.

By the summer of the new century, Amazon's stock price had dropped by more than two-thirds, and analysts began to loudly criticize Bezos for venturing into too many product categories and spreading the business too thin. The industry was filled with truths and gossip about Amazon, and everything in between. One report by BBC™ News at the time reported that the investment bank Lehman Brothers® was warning investors that Amazon was running extremely low in cash and advised them to avoid the company's stock. Rumors abounded about Amazon filing for bankruptcy or selling out to another company. Negative nicknames about the business arose, such as "Amazon.bomb" and "Amazon.toast."

At the beginning of 2001, Amazon reported a loss of $1.4 billion, but Bezos did not give up. He got back on the horse — if he ever dismounted at all — and took a different approach. He promised analysts that Amazon would report a profit by year's end by cutting expenses and restructuring the business model. 2002 was welcomed in by 1,300 layoffs or 13 percent of the workforce, closing two warehouses, shutting down a Seattle customer-service center, and eliminating all unprofitable products. Simultaneously, Bezos focused on better managing the merchandise Amazon continued to carry. This included delivering packages to postal hubs presorted by geography and developing complex algorithms to analyze items that people buy to group them in the same warehouse. An additional tactic was selling products in other companies' warehouses. Amazon switched from a specialty retailer to an online shopping portal. The site started selling products from companies such as Toys "R" Us® and Target®, and it added merchandise from smaller retailers. The emphasis was now on person-centric metrics, such as "time saved" and "money saved."

The Focus on Continuous Improvement

From the start, Bezos saw that success will come from constantly enhancing repeatable processes or "big-time process management." The marketer's role is to clearly identify what customers most want to improve and to deliver it to them. Bezos explains in the company's 2003 *Annual Report,* "Amazon's marketing strategy is designed to strengthen and broaden the Amazon.com brand name, increase customer traffic to our Web sites, encourage customers to shop in many product categories, promote repeat purchases, and develop incremental product and service revenue opportunities." As will be seen in this book, such a customer-centric approach strongly supports those who team up with Amazon to sell their own products.

Partnering with Associates

By the end of 2001, Bezos kept his promise about a personal comeback. The company reported its first profit, with fourth-quarter earnings of $5 million. This growth was backed up with additional changes. In support of its extremely high-volume business, Amazon developed a sophisticated, scalable, and reliable technology infrastructure. On its own, Amazon is extremely successful, but an important part of its business strategy now involves the company's efforts to go beyond its direct sales and to include its affiliates, which it calls Associates, and its partners.

For example, Amazon allows other online individuals and organizations to use its infrastructure to sell their products and services in return for it receiving a small commission on each sale. This arrangement proves to be beneficial for both Amazon and its Associates. An individual or business can quite easily set up an electronic storefront, which features Amazon's e-commerce capabilities. This would be much more difficult and expensive to create independently. The mechanism that Amazon uses for expanding its online e-business activities is based on its Web Services™ function. Using Web Services technologies described in this book, Amazon provides access to its technical infrastructure. There are now a variety of different ways that people like yourself can cash in on Amazon's success by leveraging the power of the e-commerce platform. In addition, through the self-publishing companies, you can publish books, movies, and music and then sell them on Amazon. As one of the vendors says in this book: "Regardless of your needs, you can find a way to make money on Amazon."

CHAPTER 1

Why Choose Amazon Over the Competition?

". . . And the reason I'm so obsessed with these drivers of the customer experience is that I believe that the success we have had over the past 12 years has been driven exclusively by that customer experience. We are not great advertisers. So we start with customers, figure out what they want, and figure out how to get it to them."

— Jeff Bezos, The New York Times, January 5, 2008

Amazon may have started affiliate programs and provided a wide variety of options for sellers throughout its history, but it definitely is not the only game in town. Many online sellers, for example, have successfully built a business with a Yahoo! store. Other Internet entrepreneurs have developed their own Web sites without affiliation to any other online company. Why then, is this book being written specifically about selling with Amazon? Why should you decide to go with Amazon versus another company — or on your own?

Presently, there are approximately one million Amazon Associates or affiliates who are earning income by referring customers to **www.Amazon.com**. Over the years, Amazon has become one of the most trusted Internet brands, with an ever-increasing range of products being offered to 59 million customers worldwide. In fact, in 2007 alone, Amazon expanded into a dozen new product categories. There are thousands of affiliate programs online, but none allow sellers to easily provide links from their sites to such a wide variety of relevant subjects as the Amazon Associates. Associates can quickly add a link to their page and begin adding revenue.

The company also continues to launch new opportunities for sellers, including the WebStore® and aStore®, which is a professional-looking online shop complete with Amazon products that you can choose to be placed on your own Web site or on a site of its own. In fact, you can have as many as 100 aStores at a time. There are affiliates who are thus simultaneously running several related Web sites. These stores can be up-and-running in a day with one low flat fee. Amazon has also released an entire range of enhancements, such as their growing number of widgets and new fulfillment options. Imagine having the opportunity to easily reach Amazon's huge customer base. In addition, Amazon's free shipping option on many sales encourages increasingly frequent purchases.

Bezos would probably say that it is wise to become part of the Amazon team because the company is doing all that it possibly can to ensure excellent customer service. This means that the businesses that have the name "Amazon" attached to them must also keep high-quality standards. In other words, "the customer comes first" consideration logically extends to the vendors of these customers. In a 2008 *Smart Money* Q&A, Bezos emphasized his view on the subject of customers:

> **SM**: Amazon has about 6 percent of all U.S. sales online. That's huge. Why muck it up with all the other businesses you've added, like manufacturing [the Kindle] and your new customer service software?
>
> **Bezos**: We are responding to customer needs.
>
> **SM**: No one asked for the Kindle.
>
> **Bezos**: True. It's not the customers' job to invent for themselves. Four years ago, we thought about extensions to our business. We took a look at what we're good at. On Kindle, we had been selling e-books for years, but you needed an electron microscope to see the sales.

The development and marketing of the Kindle™ electronic reader provides an example of how Amazon is always on the lookout for ways to turn competitive challenges into greater strengths. As the sale of books, music, and movies decline, the company can grow the electronic delivery of that content. Presently, Amazon has three active business ventures. The first is the one that they have been building from the very beginning, which services its approximately 60 million active customers. The second is the seller business, or what Amazon considers its second set of customers, which includes all proprietors from the single book seller to the large organizations like Target. The third business, which is much younger than the other two, is for the 200,000-plus developers. Regardless of which of these three entities you belong to, the overriding philosophy is Bezos' "customer-centricity." Amazon sees these three units working closely together and helping each other. For example, if Amazon did not create a huge Web infrastructure, it could not support its massive retail business which, in turn, supports the sellers. The sellers provide unique products, such as out-of-print books, which adds to Amazon's selection and continuously brings the shoppers back to the site.

Another primary strength of Amazon is what is called "the long tail," or not only selling the most popular items, but also those that have less of a demand. Amazon sellers can make more money selling a larger combined volume of less popular items. It is important to have variety and a number of different options that differentiate one business from another. In other words, Amazon helps you sell the 80 percent of your products that have lower demand, or the tail end, as well as those top 20 percent hot-selling items. People know they can turn to Amazon for those older and still excellently rated models or the non-fad merchandise. Amazon buyers can choose from millions of items that may be "on the back shelves," but still can be viewed and obtained in the virtual world.

Because Amazon is customer-centric, it keeps track of what its buyers want and will want in the future. Whenever a customer logs onto Amazon, he or she is greeted with notations such as "here are the products you last looked at," "here are some products that may be of interest," and "here are some similar products that others like yourself have viewed." A great amount of resources are devoted to following the personal online shopping habits of customers, which are compiled for promotional and helpful consumer information, including "Top Sellers" and "Just Like You."

Business Tracking System

Amazon's expertise in data collection also provides the seller with extensive information. In Seller Central™, the online interface that is used to manage the Amazon stores, sellers have the ability to easily add inventory, update product information, and retrieve orders. Sellers can also track where sales originated.

With the reports generator, you can get information from sales two months previous to those that just came in, as well as orders, cancellations, or returns. The reports are easily generated and quickly help you keep up-to-date on sales. Data analysis, which is an essential aspect of online marketing and sales, can be extremely time consuming without the proper systems in place. Amazon has the support available to help you grow your business, giving you the time to spend on determining what your customers want and giving it to them. Amazon has put a great deal of resources into making your selling more efficient, so you can handle increasing orders and more inventory changes.

Amazon prides itself in having a thorough understanding of the way that customers interact with the Web sites they visit. When new features are added, for example, customers are tracked to see if and how their behavior is changed. How are customers using the new feature? Is it helping them save time in their buying? For example, Amazon's search element called Statistically Improbable Phrases, or "SIPs," allows readers to find the most noteworthy phrases in the text of books that are within the Search

Inside!™ program. This feature allows customers to actually go "inside" a book and get an example of the work before purchasing it. To locate these SIPs, Amazon scans every Search Inside! for the desired text. When finding a phrase that occurs a large number of times in a particular book in comparison to all other Search Inside! books, it becomes a SIP. For fiction, SIPs are normally distinctive word combinations hinting at important plot elements.

The SIPs were introduced because Amazon was looking for ways to offer customers more relevant ways to view book details. When first announcing this feature, Amazon measured it in terms of customer satisfaction: Did consumers find what they needed more easily? If Amazon can improve shopping convenience, then it knows it has a success in the making. Similarly, if the company can help customers find things that they might not have thought of before, it is a hit. This is another way that the Amazon developers work closely with customer service and the sellers.

It is also very helpful that Amazon recognizes the wide diversity of its customers, from high-tech gurus to seniors who are surfing the Internet for the first time. Once again, this helps not only the customers, but the sellers as well, because they need to meet the needs of their wide variety of customers. Keeping such close track of customer numbers also helps Amazon and its sellers in preventative measures — knowing that they are doing something wrong before it becomes a major problem with customers. The online world changes amazingly fast, and customers do not only alter their buying habits on a regular basis, but they can be very fickle. Because Amazon can acquire so much data in such a short timeframe, sellers can keep in the race and win against the competition.

Which Amazon Vehicle is Best?

Selling your products on the Web allows you to reach millions of potential buyers in a cost-effective way. When the Web first was available, selling online was complex and difficult. This was especially true for small businesses that either had to hire a professional Web designer or try to personally handle the Web hosts, shopping cart providers, merchant services, marketers, and fulfillment houses.

Today, especially at Amazon, one only has to write a few words and push a few buttons, literally and figuratively. Whether you want to sell products online for the first time or enlarge your present sales, Amazon Services offers a solution. You have the opportunity to:

- Make a list of new or used products for sale

- Pare down your excess and/or outdated business inventories

- Leverage a well-established sales channel that reaches millions of customers

- Participate in an experienced, multi-node network of fulfillment centers

- Benefit from reliable credit-card processing and fraud protection services

- Use Amazon's automated customer service for regular inquiries, returns, and refunds.

- Grow a future customer base

- Take advantage of Amazon's advanced marketing and search engine optimization

- Gain from performance — fees are paid as a percentage of sales incurred

- Depend on Amazon for billing, packaging, storing, shipping, and returns

A Variable of Choices

Amazon provides sellers with several different choices that take advantage of its established sales channel, marketing vehicles, purchasing processes, search optimization, merchandising services, and payment-processing technologies. Depending on your e-commerce experience or present degree of Internet participation, you can start off slow and sell only a few items here and there, or take your present online business and expand it through Amazon's extensive online channels — or anything in between. Here are your selling options:

- **Amazon Marketplace**™ for sellers of used and new items, or those individuals with few or occasional sales

- **Amazon Pro-Merchant**™ for continuous sales of larger quantities

- **Amazon Advantage**™ for new authors, publishers, labels, and studios

- **Amazon Associates** for vendors who want to take advantage of Amazon's marketplace

- **Amazon WebStore**™ to gain further visibility with an established Web site

The remainder of this book will review each of these alternatives more specifically. Give thought to each one and determine which is best for your needs. As you will see by the case studies, many of the people who are participating with Amazon are finding new and creative ways to make additional income.

The Marketplace ("Sell Your Stuff") offers you a great way to jump into the online-selling business and reach millions of buyers with no investment. You can actually just advertise one product for sale at a time. Many people use Marketplace to sell used books in smaller quantities. Once you easily sign-up with Marketplace, you can readily price your items and get the word out to millions of Amazon's customers. In addition to helping you try out what it is like selling online, the Marketplace can help you try out a new item to see how it will be received by customers. The cost and ease is hundreds of times better than doing a full marketing research campaign. The price: You do not pay a penny until you sell an item. Then, the buyer sends the item price and shipping costs to Amazon, which deducts 6 to 15 percent from the sales price for its commission, along with a fee of $0.99 for each sale, and a variable closing fee.

Pro-Merchant is your possible next step when you already have a strong Web presence — selling approximately 50 items a week or more — and are looking for ways to expand. With Pro-Merchant, you will have the opportunity to become an Associate, allowing you to bring in additional income. You now have a way to grow your business and a place to store your products. When you sell with Pro-Merchant, you can also take advantage of Amazon's fulfillment center to store, pick, pack, and ship your products. You no longer pay the $0.99 per transaction, but do pay a monthly charge of $39.99, though you can cancel at any time. This allows you to create your own personalized storefront and items, product pages in the Amazon catalog, and listings that never expire.

Advantage is for those individuals who want to sell new books, movies, and music that they have written and/or produced, instead of promoting and selling other people's works. This is not for used works. It gives you the opportunity to market your literary or musical pieces to a very large and broad audience and is an excellent solution for the publishing field to promote and sell their items. With Advantage, the yearly cost is $29.95. This allows you to sell as many titles as you wish and the ability to manage your account. In the normal split, Amazon gets 55 percent, and you receive 45 percent from the list price. You determine the list price, which is also called suggested retail price; all payments that you receive are calculated from the list price. If Amazon lowers the sale price below the list price, Amazon pays the difference.

WebStore is a relatively new program allowing customers to create e-commerce Web sites using Amazon technology. With WebStore, you can regularly update the site quickly and easily. A Web developer does not have to be called each time a change is needed. It allows you to maintain and build your personal product and offers a perfect alternative for e-businesses that want a comprehensive solution, but do not want to give up their brand. It also provides an alternative if you have your own Web site, but your shopping cart technology is not state-of-the-art, and you spend too much time conducting auditing for false orders. Through Amazon, you can get fraud detection and protection solutions, plus other helpful technologies to grow your business. The cost is $59.99 a month, with a 7 percent commission on each item sold. The WebStore features include Amazon's "A-to-z Guarantee" on all purchases, product reviews, search engine support, and no set-up/listing fee. You can earn additional revenue by selling Amazon products on multiple WebStores with one Associates account.

Associates are the largest number of Amazon sellers. This option is best if you have a lot of traffic coming to your Web site, but not enough people want the products you are selling. This lets you get a fee every time you send someone off to Amazon and purchase a product. Many Associates are also very customer-oriented and want to give their customers the best service possible. By becoming an Amazon Associate, you can leverage your Web site's content, as well as choose from several formats for your site's links to make them fit in with the rest of the design and theme and provide a connection to Amazon where users can buy a particular item to complement your information, services, or products.

One of the best things about the Amazon Associates program is that, while you are helping users get access to the items they want on your site, you can also get additional income from utilizing Amazon's strengths. You can either receive your payment in direct cash into your bank account or, alternatively, as vouchers you can spend on Amazon. Whether you are just selling a used book twice a month or millions of dollars of products every year, Amazon can offer you the appropriate online vehicle.

Amazon strives to be the most customer-centric company, allowing users to locate nearly anything they could possibly like to purchase on the Internet. With low prices, a vast number of flexible selling options, and ease of use, Amazon maintains its growth pattern and its evolution as a top-rated e-commerce platform.

CHAPTER 2

Is the Online World For You?

Regardless of the opportunities that Amazon offers, you still need not have an online store, or publish your own book or CD and put it online. Believe it or not, even in these high-tech days, there are plenty of people who do not have their own Web site or spend all their time online. The virtual world is different than a brick-and-mortar business, and you should think about your own personal goals and interests before making a final decision on whether or not to go virtual. If you are uncertain, you can always start out small and then build up. You can sell some items that you have at home through Amazon Marketplace to get a little flavor of e-commerce and expand if you get the bug. Before you know it, you could be a virtual success.

The most important thing to remember is that running a business takes work, whether it is a traditional "offline" brick-and-mortar store or an online WebStore. Though many of the advertisers say, "Make Millions of Dollars Overnight Online," you will have to devote consistent time and effort to your e-commerce venture.

The word "consistent" is extremely important. People may say they spend 25 hours a month promoting their business and cannot understand why it is not growing as intended. They may be cramming those 25 hours into a few days of work at month's end because they knew it was important; however, this approach may or may not work. As with any business, it is much better to devote a certain amount of hours per day.

Here are some areas that you will need to consider as you move along in your business venture. As you can see, this is a step-by-step process, as is any other project you want to successfully complete. There is one surety: The more time you spend building your business, the better the chance you have at not only succeeding, but at making a significant amount of money.

- **Gaining online knowledge:** This book will help you in two important ways. The first is by helping you determine the best way to work with Amazon. You will learn that you have several options, with varying tradeoffs, and be able to decide which fits your business plan. The second is by giving you the basics about online retailing and marketing. When working with Amazon, many of the usual worries about an online business, such as designing a Web site from scratch, have significantly diminished or totally disappeared. You should still know the basics about these topics, though, because they are an integral part of e-commerce.

- **Getting to know the competition:** You need to keep up-to-date on your competitors' sites. How does their inventory compare to yours? Regularly read the copy on their Web sites and/or blogs, and even sign-up for their e-mails. Then, you will know what changes you need to make and in what ways you are superior to these other retailers.

- **Developing a business plan:** When you know what product you are going to sell, you need to set your goals and a schedule for achieving them.

- **Developing a marketing plan:** Your business plan will list the goals, and the marketing plan will help you achieve them. All marketing plans need to include a variety of promotional vehicles. This is especially true with online marketing, since no specific step-by-step plan exists. New ways to sell products are always be-ing created, and you have to keep up with them. You need to get in touch with your market and let them know how you can meet their needs.

- **Deciding on a name:** Even more so than with a brick-and-mortar business, your domain name is important from a branding and marketing standpoint. You want a name that is short, sweet, and easy to remember. Also take note that your Web address (URL) affects your search engine ranking, so you want a name that has your product included.

- **Getting your home office ready:** Even if you already have a computer, is it the right one for your online needs? Do you have an office set aside with a dedicated phone, fax machine, printer, and scanner? Do you have a backup system in case your primary one goes down? Who is going to be your online service provider?

- **Acquiring the product:** As explained later, you will have the opportunity to either purchase or make your own products and also sell them or create a store with available product. If you plan on buying the items, you need reliable vendors and confidence that the price will remain stable and not shoot up in a few months. If you are making the products, be sure that you have a large enough inventory. You do not want to keep customers waiting.

- **Sharing best practices:** You do not want to reinvent the wheel, so you can always learn from the successes and mistakes of other retailers. Networking time is worth the effort spent. Over time, you can also develop ways to promote each other.

- **Hiring technical professionals:** Find a reliable computer consultant or firm nearby to call for an office visit if an emergency arises. As long as your system is up and running, you are golden. What happens when it crashes? You need to have someone in the wings who is on-call when needed. Remember that you always need a backup plan for long-term technology problems.

- **Managing resource time:** Whether you are running this business for full- or part-time income, or for a continuous revenue stream, you do not want it to take any more time than planned. Plus, you want to make the most of the time you do have available. Time management skills will help you become aware of how you use your time to organize, prioritize, and maintain your Web site.

- **Finding personal support:** Even if you plan on running this business yourself, you need a backup person as well. This person can review any copy written for the Web site, blogs, or e-newsletters; help out at busy times; and fill in when you are not available.

Building Your Business

Creating an online Web site store, even with the ease of Amazon, does involve some setup and ongoing maintenance time. You do not want to always have the same products for sale, and you should beef up the Web site with marked-down items and sales. In addition, people do not automatically come to your site; it takes marketing and advertising. Online marketing is different from the traditional approach; there is no tried-and-true way to promote a Web site. Even the pros say that you have to use several different types of marketing to bring buyers to your store. This will require a couple of hours a day of work and, perhaps, some money to invest for product advertising.

This is also a self-motivating business, as is any privately-owned enterprise. You have no boss but yourself to motivate you to put in the necessary hours and work. You have to motivate yourself every day, set and review your own goals, and establish and follow your own schedule. You need to like logistics and organization, have good time-management skills, enjoy detail work, and be interested in the product that you are selling and promoting. If you intend to build this up as your only source of income, remember that you will be self-employed. You will not receive benefits from your employer. You will have to follow the federal and state income tax laws and find information out about a seller's permit, local licenses, and sales taxes. Depending on your arrangement with Amazon, you may or may not have to be concerned about billing, accounting, storing, and shipping your product. You are responsible for finding and purchasing your own product and maintaining a Web site to display it.

Many people are naturally 9-to-5 employees; others are naturally, independently business-minded. Both of these are important in the business world; you have to decide where your interests fall. Even if you intend for this to be "found money" or extra income, you will need to have the same skills and interests as someone who goes into this full-time. This preparation time includes learning some business and retail basics as well. If you have never run a business, it is important to take a course in or research various business topics, such as merchandising, accounting, and marketing. Also, study product trends; what you decide to sell is most important. It could be something you know well or are interested in, or a product that is becoming more popular with time. Be careful, though: You do not want to sell an item that is growing in sales, but does not interest you.

As always, businesses do not succeed overnight. No one just hops on the Web and makes a large amount of money. Your competition, as with brick-and-mortar stores, will continue to grow, and it will take several years to build a reputation and sizeable customer base. Finally, the biggest difference between off- and online stores: Even when you are part of many online communities, and you e-mail, blog, chat, write in forums, talk on the telephone, and even make some good online friends, you will not personally see people on a one-on-one basis every day as you do in a brick-and-mortar business. This is a people business, but a virtual people business.

A Number of Plusses for Online Business

On the other hand, the advantages to Web retailing are many. An e-commerce shopping cart gives you the opportunity to make sales without being present in person. Because it is so easy to set up your Web site design and selling features, you can put together an online store in literally minutes without having to hire an expensive design firm. All surveys report that e-commerce will continue to boom in the near future. The forecast stands between 20 to 40 percent a year, depending on the industry. The highlights of an online business include:

- **A 24/7 presence online**: Your store never closes. Go to work in your pajamas. Work at night after the children go to sleep. Get up early with the birds. It does not matter.

- **A global reach**: The world is becoming "flatter" all the time, with people everywhere on the globe interfacing on a regular basis. You never know who is going to want your product — from Louisville, Kentucky, to Nagoya, Japan.

- **Different interests and tastes**: Similar to the point above, you do not have to be dependent on the likes and dislikes of people in your immediate selling area. People throughout the world have many different interests.

- **Reduced advertising and marketing costs**: Regardless of where you sell, there will be a marketing budget. Especially if you connect with a marketing-oriented company such as Amazon, you can more cost-effectively reach a much larger pool of potential buyers specifically looking for your type of product. With paid and non-paid marketing tools such as blogs, pay-per-click, and search engine optimization (SEO) methods, you can lead targeted traffic to your site at a relatively low cost.

- **Traffic measuring techniques**: You can determine when visitors buy and what they buy, and also what makes them come to your Web site, stay for a while and, most importantly, come back. With market research information such as this coming in on a regular basis, you can continually update your business strategy to make necessary changes to your shopping cart, improve sales with niche markets, and update your online catalog based on the emerging data trends.

- **A wealth of support information**: This is available to you through the helpline at Amazon and the many different Amazon forums that range from "new sellers" to "success stories." You can ask seasoned sellers your questions to avoid reinventing the wheel. Similarly, these are not the only forums that you can plug into. There is a myriad of information online that offers tips about selling.

The decision to sell online will depend on numerous intimate facts about your personal goals, work habits, interests, type of industry you are looking to enter, and resources available to you. The case studies in this book will also give you a better idea on how other people made this decision and some of the successes and challenges they have had along the way.

Amazon will provide you with a great deal of customer service, product, marketing, and operational support if you do decide to take the online route. However, you need to do your homework about the Internet world if you plan on starting a successful business. Just as you would a brick-and-mortar business, you need to write a business plan with a business description, product line, name, target audience, timeline, costs, marketing strategy, accounting, and taxes. You also have to do as much reading and learning about virtual selling as possible. Since it is such a fast-paced, ever-changing environment, you will want to be well-prepared before having to face a lot of the general business challenges that will come your way.

Niches are becoming increasingly important online. People are looking for specific information and products about very narrow areas of interest. To help you determine the products you will sell, you definitely have to get to know the online marketplace. In addition to checking out Web sites through Amazon and other venues, you should be reading blogs, forums, and social networks. You will find out a lot more about the people who will be buying from your site and, more importantly, about their needs. Make a list of e-commerce Web sites that you like and why. Read tips from other sellers, such as those in the case studies in this book. Other people who are selling online have a great deal to offer you, and most of them will gladly answer your questions. The forums that Amazon has will also be very helpful.

You are particularly looking for stores that customers will appreciate because of their easy-to-navigate design; combination of relevant information and product; convenience and ease of use; and competitive price. By acquainting yourself with Google® AdWords℠, you will find out the topics and Associate Web sites that are leaders in the field.

Today's customers are interested in making informed decisions. They do not want products just foisted on them, but rather want to look at and compare the options. They want more information on the products they buy. Selling online successfully means to provide this information and the means for the consumers to make their own decisions. Smart marketers can customize messages to different audiences. Interactive marketing, which focuses on the demographic and psychographic characteristics of the consumer, makes the connection with the potential customers much more immediate. This is why interactive marketing is seen so regularly online. It is used for prospecting new customers, customer service, creating a conversation with customers, and ongoing promotions. You store huge amounts of information, but only give each customer the desired information.

Your customers also want the information they desire when they desire it. This is another plus of interactive marketing. Companies can provide information and be available to respond to questions 24/7 to compete globally.

CHAPTER 3

Get Ready to Start

Have you always wanted to open a store? Regardless if you open a brick-and-mortar or online store, you have to do your homework before hanging up your sign or, more appropriately, opening your Web site. The more time and thought you give beforehand, the smoother the transition will be. Also, take note that you may not be paying for the overhead of a brick-and-mortar store, but you will have inventory and some form of monthly charges for your Web site maintenance. Unfortunately, thousands of people launch their new e-commerce businesses and soon realize that something is not complete. For example, a couple months down the pike when traffic needs to pick up, they have no money left for marketing purposes.

When opening an online store, you will not get into your car and go to your retail store. You will, however, want to set up an area that is your designated place of business. To avoid distractions, you might consider making this area secluded from the family and household pets. As with any business, you are officially working when you are in your office. Unless an emergency arises, you should not be interrupted by some household need. It is important to establish this practice from the beginning, as working from your house can become difficult if there is not a separation between home life and work life.

Physical Equipment and Hardware to Get You Started

Although your actual business will be conducted online, you need up-to-date equipment and technology to accomplish the work. You have to consider hardware and software requirements.

Your computer will be your most essential piece of hardware. You do not need a computer with all the bells and whistles, especially if you will be relying on Amazon's own Web capacity, abilities, and services. With the price of computers going down every year, you can get an excellent deal for your money. The most important issue is reliability, as you need to be up and running 24/7. If, and when, your system crashes, your doors close — and your customers are locked out.

You may already have a computer. It may be completely outdated if it is older than a few years. If your computer has truly been a trusty workhorse, have a systems specialist evaluate its performance capabilities to ensure it is capable of handling the tasks necessary for your business. If you are just in this for some personal enjoyment and to make a few extra dollars of "play money" each month, you can use an older and slower computer that has been around for years, or even one at the local library. Take note, though: This means, once again, that you have to establish a specific schedule and rely on someone else's capability. Even libraries have a problem with computer networks going offline.

Of course, numerous companies sell computers, and each have their reasons why theirs is the best. Read computer magazine articles that rate the various brand names for reliability. Also, there are hundreds of online forums and chat groups you can join where other online merchants will offer their suggestions on the system that works best. Remember that, although everyone is selling online, you may have different needs.

Some e-commerce enterprises may be considerably dependent on Web site layout and graphics if they do their own Web site design. Other Web sites may have a high volume of products and require an extensive database. Some other vendors may rely mostly on Amazon's Web Services capabilities and only need a basic model to upload product descriptions and follow sales on Amazon's site. Once you determine how and what you plan on selling, you need to make a checklist of the computer capabilities that are most important to your line of work. The computer will be your essential connection to the Internet and your customers. Processor speed, the size of the hard drive, and the operating system will be of interest to you.

System Recommendations

The following are minimum recommendations for your computer-related requirements:

| Processor | Intel® Pentium Dual Core® processor, 2 GHz |
| RAM | Minimum 2, 3, or 4 GB recommended |

Hard Drive	500 GB
Operating System	Windows Vista® Home Premium or Windows XP® Professional
Software	Microsoft® Office 2007
Screen	17-22" LCD flat screen monitor, Super VGA (800x600 minimum)
Graphics Card	GPU from ATI™ or Nvidia® with at least 128 MB of on-board memory
Drive	CD-ROM and/or DVD-ROM
Storage	120 GB
Photo Software	Corel® PaintShop Photo™ or similar program
Printer	All-in-one laser printer, scanner, copier, fax
Internet Connection	DSL/Cable, broadband, or high-speed modem
Digital Camera	Minimum 8 megapixels

Here are some of the basics that you should consider when setting up your online business office:

Processor (CPU)

The CPU, or the Central Processing Unit, is often called the computer's brain. The CPU completes the calculations and answers the commands when a program is run. The CPU speed, which is measured in MHz (megahertz) or GHz, is very important. You do not necessarily need the fastest machine on the market. It depends on how you will be using your computer in terms of graphics, music, and video.

Memory

A common misunderstanding is that the terms "memory" and "hard drive space" are interchangeable rather than two different entities. Hard drive space refers to the existing amount of storage capacity on the computer's hard disk(s). Memory, instead, means the amount of random access memory (RAM) installed in the computer. RAM significantly impacts the computer's operating speed. When starting a home-based business, you want to know that your computer can handle the hard tasks. Getting as much RAM as possible will allow the computer to easily do the necessary work.

Hard Drive

A hard drive is a mass storage device located in all personal computers for storing permanent information, including the operating system, programs, and user files. This data can be erased and/or overwritten. If you are using a large number of complex graphics on your Web site, then consider that you need more storage. If need be, you can always add on an external hard drive. An external hard drive can provide a safety net for important documents, allowing you to back up all items on your internal hard drive. The external hard drive can become a lifesaver in the case of an internal system crash. External hard drives are available in multiple different storage amounts. It is recommended that you purchase one with 500 GB of storage space.

Upgrade

When you purchase a computer, make sure that you can upgrade components like the RAM, hard drive, and backup storage devices. Because technology changes so quickly, you need reliable upgrade options. Most computers have DVD- and CD-writing capabilities, which are helpful when backing up programs and files.

Notebook or Desktop?

In the past, desktop computers have been emphasized over laptop computers because you have been able to get more bang for your buck with a desktop PC. Many laptops are just as powerful as desktops, but they were a bit pricey. However, the costs of laptops are now coming down, and it is making more sense to have a docking station that your laptop can fit into to expand its functionalities when you do not have it on the road. This is an especially helpful option when you do need your computer for off-site presentations. On the other hand, if you do all of your work from your home office, there is no need to look further than a good, low-cost, workhorse desktop PC.

Peripherals

The cost of monitors is tumbling. You can find a 17- to 22-inch liquid crystal display (LCD) monitor for a reasonable price. The older cathode ray tube (CRT) boxes are no longer being sold on most models, although they are still quite functional. The main advantage of the CRT over the LCD was the color rendering. However, unless you plan on doing a great deal of intricate graphic design work, a LCD screen will be a much better option due to its weight and size. LCD screens also tend to produce less eye strain.

You also need a printer. This does not have to be the best and the highest grade, but one that works well with the newer operating systems. Printer prices have come down, but ink cartridges have steadily gone higher. You can save money by refilling empty ink cartridges yourself, using kits, or taking the empties to a business that specializes in refilling cartridges. Scanners are available as stand-alone units, and they are often included as part of an all-in-one unit (a printer, copier, scanner, and fax machine). You need a fax machine for sending and receiving a wide variety of documents and images. In order to keep up with technological advances, you might consider a printer that has wireless capabilities. This will allow you to print from your wireless laptop or desktop computer and can also be helpful for connecting several computers on a network.

A digital camera is a piece of photographic equipment that you can use to take pictures of your products. These pictures can be uploaded to your Web site. Photos of your products are not only a good selling strategy, but often required on auction sites. Look for the megapixel count and also the memory type and size. Do not get a higher megapixel count than you need — not typically more than 8mp — for Web site work; the photos will just take up more room in storage space.

Phone and Internet Service

For IRS tax purposes, building business credit, and privacy needs, you need to have a business-dedicated phone line. You do not want to use the home phone. You can get an Internet-based phone or a traditional phone line for a low monthly price. With bundled services, you can choose from cable Internet and phone service packages. Most packages offer phone, TV, and Internet service, but you may be able to pick and choose your desired services. A bundled package from a telephone company will consist of satellite TV, landline phone, digital subscriber loop (DSL) Internet, and possibly cellular service. A cable television company will likely offer cable Internet and digital phone service. Speed of downloading and choosing a reliable service is essential.

Wireless Capabilities

Flexibility is one of the plusses of an online business. If you plan on accessing your computer from different locations within or outside of your home, you may want to consider a docking system that allows both laptops and PC to connect to the Internet wirelessly. Most new computers automatically come with wireless cards built into the system. You will have to buy an Internet router to wirelessly access the Internet. This will allow you to access the Internet from anywhere within your home, including in bed or out by the pool. This is a perfect option for people who have other responsibilities around the home during work hours, allowing you to not be confined to a desk. Having a wireless card installed in your laptop will also allow you to access the Internet on-the-go in designated Wi-Fi locations (such as your local coffee shop or bookstore).

CHAPTER 4

What is the Best Product to Sell?

It is important to spend some time thinking about your product. If you have a definite interest in something, such as jewelry or DVDs, follow it. You can specialize in a certain niche areas that will bring in the most sales, as both of these are large product lines. Too many people just jump in and go with a product they think will sell well and find that they do not understand the product, or do not enjoy selling it.

Also, give thought to finding a product that is always needed and will provide a steady stream of income over a longer period of time. You may not make huge sales at the beginning, but over time, your business will grow. It is best to decide on a product that genuinely interests you or provides a significant amount of enjoyment; by doing this, you will enjoy spending the time it takes to learn about your product, your customers, and your main competitors and their prices. The product should fit well with your interests, and, at the same time, it should match with the product or niche industry.

Ask yourself these questions before starting:

- Do you have a basic skill, personal passion, or interest that can readily be sold online?

- Is there anything in your past career path that may help you sell a present product?

- Do you know of a product that you can readily obtain from your local area?

- Are you considering a fad item that will sell hot and then disappear, or one that will be needed for years to come?

- Is this an item that can be sold on Amazon? Have you carefully researched this product line on the site?

- Is your potential product only of interest seasonally, or throughout the year?

- What do you expect will be the profit margin for the product ideas you are exploring, and is there any room for future price negotiations?

- Can the items be readily and easily drop-shipped, stocked, handled, packaged, and shipped out again?

- How difficult is it to purchase the item from a vendor?

- Are you going to make the product, assemble it, or purchase as-is? How are you going to brand the product as your own?

- Do you have a location to store products and prepare them for shipping?

- Is the product easily marketed because it is well-recognized? Or, is it a more unique item that will take additional marketing efforts?

- Who is your target consumer, and what are some of the different types of people who are most likely to buy the products you will potentially sell?

- How competitive is the potential product market or industry? Is it open for additional sellers, or is it saturated?

- Is there a special niche to this product that will give you a way to market the product differently from the major competitors?

The main reason that you should have a passion for — or at least an interest in — the product is that you have to know what you are selling inside and out. To purchase, market, sell, and respond to consumer questions, you will need to know everything there is about your product. You also need to keep up with the product as it evolves, especially if it is electronic. When dealing with merchandising companies, you want to make sure that you are being treated fairly and that the prices you pay are accurate.

Keeping abreast of the industry also makes you an expert in the field, and from a marketing and public relations standpoint, this is what consumers want to see. As it is universally accepted in present-day business, knowledge is a product in and of itself. Later in this book, this concept of product knowledge will once again be covered.

As noted above, there is a considerable amount of information online. Granted, you have to separate the good Web sites from the bad, and those that are selling a product from those that are actually providing relevant information. There are many business publications and organizations that provide sound information, and there are also books, trade journals, and newspaper articles. Social networks, communities, blogs, and forums offer valuable information. Do not forget about the traditional means of obtaining information, such as courses (now many of which are online) and mentors (for example, SCORE) or counselors. Most of these counselors have had brick-and-mortar companies, but they can provide a wealth of information. Again, you will hear comments from several different viewpoints, and it will be up to you to take what is relevant to your own needs. The decisions you make will be based on your own personal resources of time and budget.

You do not want to sell a product on Amazon that is totally saturated. Yet, you do not want to sell one where there are few products in demand. Competitors in this respect are a good thing. They are actually doing the marketing for you, as they are acquainting the consumers with the product. If there were no competition, it would be up to you to create a need, which is quite difficult. It is essential to know whether or not your products are in demand and to what extent. Unless it is a fad and you expect a fast change in supply and demand, you do not want to start selling a product where the sources will start to dry up because of a lack of ongoing consumer demand.

For many reasons, you need to clearly define your target audience and learn as much about these individuals as you possibly can. Knowing your potential customers not only helps when finding products to sell; it also helps when you are designing your Web site, developing a blog, and marketing the product down the line. Remember that interests are always changing. Reviewing Amazon's Web site may provide some help with your product choice. Although you may be able to determine your wider interest, such as electronics, jewelry, or pet products, perhaps you have not been able to decide on a niche or smaller area. Through several different vehicles, Amazon provides insight into what is "hot" and what is not. A word of caution: Just because an item is hot today does not mean that it will retain its popularity over time. Once you see which products are selling best, continue to do your homework regarding future trends in the marketplace.

Let us say, for example, that you were considering the area of small kitchen appliances. You may have always enjoyed cooking, may even have taken some classes in cuisine, and have noticed the increased interest on television about this subject. However, the area of small kitchen appliances is very wide. Go to Amazon and click on "Kitchen and Dining," and then on "Small Appliances." On the top menu, click "Best Sellers." This will bring up, on the left panel, "Hot New Releases," "Most Gifted," "Most Wished For," and "Movers and Shakers." The best-selling new and future releases in small appliances, as with other products, are updated hourly. At the time of this writing, this brings up several different blenders, yogurt makers, deep fryers, and microwave ovens. Reading the customer reviews about these products will provide additional information. At the end of the year, Amazon also releases the highest-selling products. This market research is also a valuable tool in helping you make your decision.

Create Your Wish List

The "Wish List" is a personalized list of everything a person or organization would like to own that is now being sold on Amazon. "Movers & Shakers" tracks products that have significantly increased in sales. It is also updated hourly to reflect real-time buying trends and tells you a great deal about collective buying habits of Amazon's shoppers.

Finding the Right Source

When deciding on a product line, you also have to consider the way that you will be purchasing the items. Many products are sold primarily overseas, and there are few or no U.S. distributors. That can be problematic, even though the prices may be lower. Also, the sources you contact to purchase existing products should offer the items at a price that will enable you to remain competitive with others who may sell the same or similar products. Find the best possible prices from as many reputable sources as possible and narrow your choices from there, based on time in business, track record, customer service, shipping time, and bulk discounts. You need to do some deeper research into who manufactures, distributes, and sells the products to retailers. Who are industry suppliers, who are their usual customers, and how does the purchasing system work? At first, you will want to purchase from the distributor or wholesale supplier, or even from other retailers.

Once you get your feet in the water, you may want to set up an arrangement directly with the manufacturer. When you cut out the middleman, the cost will naturally be lower. Conversely, there are a lot of filters that a vendor goes through to get the product that saves you possible aggravation. Rather than have product sent directly to you for storage, you can use Amazon to store it for you; there will be more information on this strategy later. A drop-ship is when the products you purchase from the vendor go directly to Amazon; they then store the product for you and package and ship the product when it is sold. Of course, you can create or manufacture the item yourself. This adds considerable work, but you are carving out a customized niche in your product line.

Amazon Stores Your Products

amazon.com

Amazon, Amazon.com and the Amazon.com logo are registered trademarks of Amazon.com, Inc. or its affiliates.

Trying to choose the right product is not easy, but the most important thing is to decide on one that is the right fit for you personally and for your business mission and goals. Pick a product that is affordable and accessible to you and also has a competitive price. Success in an online business not only is based on how well you sell your product; it also depends considerably on your ability to find and purchase the product at the right price. You may start your Amazon business with merchandise from local liquidators, closeout sales, government auctions, newspaper classifieds, or even leftovers from garage sales. To start a real niche business, with the same product line all the time, it is important to locate a reliable source supplier, which could be a manufacturer, distributor, or wholesaler. You can find the contact information online.

A number of suppliers are unable to fulfill small orders and will not provide service to small retailers. Especially for those just starting with Amazon, the minimum amount of products to buy is way too large to handle. Yet, although the manufacturer will not directly service retailers, it will give you product information and the names of its wholesalers and distributor companies, which can better help meet your needs. For some types of items, you are better off going to a trade or industry show to find a supplier. This will also allow you to see what is coming down the road.

Search for Web sites of exhibition centers in large cities near you and sign up for a couple of trade shows in your product line. You want the participants to be distributors and wholesalers, not manufacturers. Again, not all suppliers will work with small orders, so this will allow you to meet a large number of contacts in a short period of time. It considerably cuts down your research time.

Do not forget about the traditional trade journals in your related field. Suppliers are normally listed, or are selling merchandise in these books. Many trade journals actually publish an annual book of products and also the associated manufacturers and suppliers. They have reports on trends in the industry and the latest information on new products, major players, industry events, and classified sections. Your local business and trade associations also have meetings and materials, in addition to exceptional networking opportunities. You may find suppliers who are actually looking for individuals such as yourself to help them promote their products. There are also companies that are marketing their services to meet the needs of small business retailers. For example, **www.Importers.com** is a major online business-to-business (b2b) trade company that provides a searchable, online directory of more than 200,000 international firms and Internet resources to buy and sell products online. The company helps buyers and distributors find new international suppliers, manufacturers, and wholesalers to help promote their products.

Most of the consumer products you will get from suppliers will be made in another country. Today, with the reach of globalization, importing products is a great deal easier than it was in previous years. Large global sellers are located in most major countries.

Here are some tips for successfully importing products:

- Find several suppliers through online sources or by contacting a specific country's trade commission.

- Contact the suppliers to see if they carry your product and the quantity you have to purchase. Remember that many of these suppliers may also sell through Amazon or with other retailers through Amazon, and may be competing with you.

- Before making any final deals, have them send you several samples to make sure that they meet your exact specifications. You do not want to be surprised when you open up that first shipment.

- The fee will include the cost of the product, as well as packing, shipping, insuring, covering customs and excise duty, financing, and handling charges.

- If you can, go to the supplier's outlet. Get to know the company firsthand. Ask for the names of references of retailers who are presently working with them. Once again, through forums, you can do your due diligence. You do not want to be burned.

- Learn all you can about shipping and the specific rules for exporting goods in the country that sells your product. Talk with a customs broker to learn about necessary regulations for shipping and exporting.

- Find out information on seasonal production changes, possible reasons for a slowdown of products, and shipping times. Have a backup plan in place if an emergency arises and you cannot get the product when needed.

CHAPTER 5

Selling in the Amazon Marketplace

Amazon Marketplace is especially suitable for those people who have loads of "stuff" in decent condition in their garages, basements, attics, and around the house that they want to get rid of. As noted earlier, Marketplace is a great way to introduce yourself to online selling and make additional income. According to Amazon, here is what you can sell on Marketplace:

- Any item that is located in Amazon's category listing.

- Something you would like to see listed, along with other similar items that Amazon is selling now. If a customer enters a name of a product and does not want the full price and sees your substitute — you just may sell it.

- A product you can list that is in a "new," "collectible," "refurbished," or "used" condition.

- Anything that you want to ship yourself to the buyer.

- All merchandise that you would like to go through Amazon and then have the payment go on to you.

- Anything on which you want Amazon to get a commission charge.

Here is a list of what you cannot sell through Marketplace:

- Any promotional books, music, videos, or DVDs prior to release for distribution or sale.

- Merchandise that is unauthorized and unlicensed.

- Any items that you copied yourself that are trademarked.

Amazon started as a bookstore, and the Marketplace is still a recommended place to sell used books. Yet now, buyers can find nearly everything on Amazon, above and beyond books.

Sellers can list products in numerous categories, including:

- Sports and fitness
- Kids and baby
- Clothing
- Jewelry
- Home and garden
- Food and household
- Tools and automotive

- Computer and office
- Consumer electronics
- Toys and video games
- Traditional books, music, DVDs, and videos

amazon.com

Amazon, Amazon.com and the Amazon.com logo are registered trademarks of Amazon.com, Inc. or its affiliates.

Anyone 18 years or older can sell products on Amazon. It is incredibly easy to get started in the selling game. If you have something to sell, you post it on the site in the appropriate category, and Amazon takes a commission — if, and only if, someone buys it. You are giving Amazon a cut because the company is providing the location and the opportunity to sell to millions of people. Marketplace is the selling vehicle for every person. Anyone can use it, and it is quite simple to set up. Amazon Marketplace allows you to sell your new, used, collectible, and refurbished items alongside Amazon's new ones. But Marketplace is not an auction, as you set the price of every item listed. Keep in mind that the more competitive the price, the faster it will sell.

Marketplace is the perfect selling venue for sellers who would rather not have a Web site and do not have three million widgets to sell. Here are the selling basics:

- You can list anything that is located in the Amazon catalog.

- Your item may be highlighted next to the same item that Amazon is selling new. When searching for a baby stroller, a customer will immediately go to that category on Amazon and just may see your product on the same page.

- You will be placing your items in a variety of categories, depending on what you are selling and the condition of that item.

Condition of Item

Amazon expects merchants to label their items in a specific manner. For example, here are specifications for labeling a computer:

- **New:** "New" means precisely, perfectly "new." All items have to be brand-new, in unopened, unsealed packages with their original packaging materials, peripherals, and software. If there is a manufacturer's warranty, it still is with the packaging and will apply.

- **Refurbished:** Merchandise has been professionally repaired and cleaned to working order, including an inspection to meet the manufacturer's quality control guidelines. The item may or may not be in its original packaging, and the warranty from the manufacturer or restorer may apply to the item and therefore might still be found inside the packaging.

- **Like New:** Similar to the new merchandise, this is unused and in brand-new condition. Although the original plastic wrap may not be on the item, the software is as originally packed, and no signs of wear are anywhere on the packaging.

- **Very Good:** This would be a computer that may have been used to some extent and shows minor signs of wear, but it still is in excellent original working condition, and it includes the instructions and software.

- **Good:** It is possible to see the signs of prior, consistent use, but it remains in quality condition and perfect working order. Included inside are the instructions from the original item and software in satisfactory condition. Overall, it is in good shape.

- **Acceptable:** The computer has been used with noticeable outward wear, such as scratches and dents, but it still is in perfect working condition. It may not be in the original box and have instructions, but the software is included.

Signing Up for Marketplace

It is easy to register for Marketplace. You will see a "Sell on Amazon" link on the bottom of Amazon's homepage, or in one of the links on the left column. From here, it is a four-step process.

1 List your items

2 Get orders

3 Ship

4 Get paid

amazon.com

Amazon, Amazon.com and the Amazon.com logo are registered trademarks of Amazon.com, Inc. or its affiliates.

There is an easy registration page, which asks for your e-mail address for notification of sale, bank account for payment deposit, and shipping address. As soon as you sign up as an Amazon seller, the "ships-from" location automatically becomes your billing address. If necessary, you can make changes to this location on the "Store Setting" page in your "Seller Account." You will be asked for a ZIP or postal code if you enter the U.S. or Canada as your country. When a product is listed, the buyer will see the ships-from location and can estimate about how long it will be before the item will arrive.

Amazon expects that you will mail all products within two business days after the sale was made, and the item needs to arrive within four to 14 business days after the shipping date for normal shipping, and two to six days for expedited mailings. International shipments should arrive within three to six weeks (or later, if there are customs delays). A buyer outside the U.S. can purchase your item only if you select the "International Shipping" option. Amazon will give you a shipping credit to help cover shipping costs when you make a sale on Marketplace. How much you receive will be based on the item that is for sale. The buyer pays a specific shipping fee when purchasing the product, and this is passed on to you.

When you list a specific item for sale, you will be asked for the condition and description. Find the category for the item you are selling. If it is not listed, there is another range of items in the category called "Everything Else." You do not have to take a picture of your item. You determine a price level and how you want to handle shipment. When you make a sale, the transaction is handled completely by Marketplace. You do not need to set up a PayPal® account or other online financial account. Amazon will deposit the money directly to the bank account you listed every two weeks, and Amazon will notify you by e-mail when an order has been placed. You need to immediately pack up the item and ship to the customer as ordered, unless you have made an agreement with Amazon to send out your items by fulfillment.

Shipping Your Product

As soon as you receive an e-mail from Amazon notifying you that an item has been sold, the product needs to be shipped to the customer. Customer service is not only the most important aim of Amazon; it should be for you, too. If you want to have repeat business from a customer and maintain a high rating with other potential buyers, you must always keep service in mind. Rather than waiting for additional sales before you go to the post office, be committed to going any day you receive an e-mail, as prompt delivery is very important to customers. They will rate you well or poorly depending on the number of days it took to receive their item. You will be sending most, if not all, of your packages through the United States Postal Service (USPS), as there are no additional fees as there are with United Parcel Service (UPS) or Federal Express (FedEx).

Send your buyers an e-mail confirmation that the item is on its way. You can use the "Sold, Ship Now" e-mail supplied by Amazon. You can also print out a packing slip to include in the package. Buyers must contact sellers no later than 14 days after receipt to advise them of product issues and arrange for a return. Returns must be sent within 30 days after shipment. Marketplace sellers must take back returns even when the product is precisely as was advertised. Upon receipt of the item, you will issue a refund to your buyer. When you do not hold responsibility for the product's return, the buyer will pay for the return shipping costs. You are able to get a refund with your "Manage Your Orders" tool, which refunds the buyer and credits your account.

Product Categories/Commissions and Pricing

- **Amazon Kindle** = 15 percent
- **Automotive parts and accessories** = 12 percent
- **Camera and photo** = 8 percent
- **Cell phones and accessories** = 15 percent
- **Computers** = 6 percent
- **Electronic items** = 8 percent
- **Items in the "Everything Else" store** = 15 percent
- **Musical instruments** = 12 percent
- **Watches** = 13 percent
- **All other product lines** = 15 percent

amazon.com

Amazon, Amazon.com and the Amazon.com logo are registered trademarks of Amazon.com, Inc. or its affiliates.

There will be a shipping charge added to anything sold through Marketplace, and you are not permitted to benefit from Amazon's provision for free shipping when the order is for $25 or more. The majority of Marketplace products need to be at or below the Amazon price. When it is time to input the price for your product, Amazon will tell you essential information, such as the maximum price, recommended cost due to the condition of the item, and the average cost of those pre-orders that are still pending. Marketplace items will appear on Amazon product detail pages.

If Amazon does not carry the item, then you must go to the "Create a Product Detail Page."

Keeping Track of Sales

Amazon offers Marketplace vendors a number of different tools to keep track of their past and potential sales, such as status of accounts, buyers, and refunds. With the "Manage Orders" feature, you have a customizable overview of your orders. This tool ensures you the ability to have a listing of all of the orders within a given date range, or you can look for specific orders. You can also sort by the "Shipping Service" column in order to see which items need to be sent out first. With "Order Details," you can view the date of purchase and shipping, shipping address, and other specific details about the merchandise sold. A link sends you to the buyers' page to see the profile of individual buyers and refund orders. You will also find a summary of the payments received and processed, in addition to a transaction history of total sales, invoices, and refunds.

This report also contains any information concerning the "A-to-z Guarantee," which is one of Amazon's strongest selling points with buyers. It allows them to file a claim if the item received is different than what is expected from the merchant's advertisement. Amazon customers are also asked to leave feedback on the vendors who sent them merchandise. A seller can be rated from one to five stars, with five being best. This rating will appear alongside the name of their business.

Feedback Manager

Use the Feedback Manager to track buyer satisfaction with your service. You can view short- and long-term metrics, as well as detailed feedback entries, including buyer names and order IDs. Click the Or~~~~~~~~~~~~~~~thin the Manage Orders section of your Seller Account. Learn more.

Review Your Performance
Get a quick overview of feedback metrics.

Feedback Rating: ★★★★★

		30 days	90 days	365 days	Lifetime
	Positive	97%	98%	96%	96%
Check Your Profile	Neutral	3%	2%	2%	2%
Quickly link to the buyer view.	Negative	0%	0%	1%	2%
	Count	35	93	353	835

This feedback information is available to buyers. See how your feedback displays on Amazon.

View Current Feedback

Expand the view
See 50 ratings per page.

Respond to Feedback
Buttons are easy to find below buyer comments.

View all your feedback

Date	Rating	Comments		Order ID	Rater	Rater Role
8/29/08	5	This is a g~~~~ ~~~~ printer and it arrived quickly! Would buy from this seller ag~~~. RESPOND		058-5305764-3334922	John Buyer	Buyer
8/29/08	5	I was thrilled find a copy of this old movie and in good condition e~~~~ y as described. Thanks! ~~~~~~		058-265~ 585413		
8/29/08	3	~~eek after classe~ ~~s lots of highlig~ ~~sponse: Buyer should ha~ ng. The book was listed in "U~ not~ as being heavier in early chapters.~ REMOVE RESPONSE		~8-8799964- ~224721	Bea Customer	Buyer

Contact Your Buyer
Use the Communication Manager.

Remove a Response
You can quickly remove your comments.

View Order Details
Go to the Manage Your Orders view.

amazon.com

Amazon, Amazon.com and the Amazon.com logo are registered trademarks of Amazon.com, Inc. or its affiliates.

Some Amazon Marketplace vendors use Amazon's Services Order Notifier (ASON), a desktop application with Microsoft Windows. When ASON is running, it regularly searches Amazon to retrieve any new orders that have come in. ASON maintains an order history of the last 30 days. It also provides the details of each order and prints a shipping label and packing slip for items to be shipped. If you keep ASON running during the day, it will keep orders up-to-date.

Should You Consider a Pro-Merchant Account?

The Amazon Pro-Merchant subscription is optional — you do not need a paid subscription to begin selling on Amazon. Yet, as noted, if you sell enough items — about 20 products a month — you may be better off with a Pro-Merchant account, as it is geared toward frequent or high-volume sellers. The cost for becoming a Pro-Merchant is $39.99 a month. According to the Amazon Web site, the Pro Merchant subscription allows you to tap into Amazon's "Seller Central" and take advantage of inventory reports that allow you to review orders that have been placed and listings that are currently open. Instead of paying the 99-cent-per-sale Marketplace fee, you are charged a 6 to 15 percent commission, as well as the variable closing fee. If an item is not sold through Marketplace within 60 days, the listing is closed. The seller receives an e-mail from Amazon confirming that the listing has ended, and a reminder of how to relist if desired. Pro-Merchant listings remain on the Amazon site until they are sold or the Pro-Merchant removes them.

As a Pro-Merchant, you can take advantage of the "inventory loader" service and upload thousands of listings in a single file, then alter, update, or eliminate them on any spreadsheet program, such as Microsoft Excel®. You can also choose from four different inventory reports. The "open listings" report includes everything that is being offered for sale at the time the report is generated. The "open listings lite and liter" report is scaled down from the standard report in order for you to quickly update the inventory you have listed. You can also access the "canceled listings" report for withdrawn items and the "sold listings" report for all sales made.

Pro-Merchant Marketplace Fulfillment Center

Amazon offers an effective way for e-commerce merchants to benefit from Amazon's services for shipping products. With the Fulfillment Web Service (FWS), sellers have the ability to take advantage of Amazon's fulfillment centers and shipping expertise. Sellers are able to ask that their order instructions be sent to Amazon in order to have Amazon fulfill their specific customer orders. The merchants can inventory their own products in the centers and, with an easy-to-use Web service interface, can fulfill product orders. As Amazon notes, "The purpose is to be able to ship a product with a simple Web service call. By making it possible for merchants to further automate their e-commerce and fulfillment efforts, Amazon is demonstrating its commitment to selling the company's e-commerce infrastructure." Amazon designed its FWS to integrate with Fulfillment by Amazon® (FBA), Amazon's fulfillment service that was started in 2006, by allowing merchants the ability of fulfilling items programmatically. In addition, Amazon offers a separate fulfillment program for its Advantage Program.

Amazon and other retailers are increasingly putting an emphasis on fulfillment logistics, which is what happens after the order is placed. Quality fulfillment — when the right product is placed in the right box and shipped to the right place at the right time — is an essential aspect of selling online. The Web offers unlimited opportunities to reach consumers, but it also introduces new challenges. Web merchants find that product fulfillment — picking, packing, and shipping small quantities of merchandise through parcel post vendors — can become extremely resource-intensive.

They often have to rely on third-party fulfillment operations to meet their shipping demands. It can be an overwhelming task that many small businesses would rather not take on.

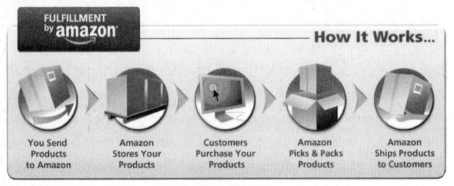

amazon.com

Amazon, Amazon.com and the Amazon.com logo are registered trademarks of Amazon.com, Inc. or its affiliates.

Frequently, e-commerce retailers are so busy with their front-end business that they do not give as much thought as they should to the back office, including this area of fulfillment and distribution — a feature that is essential to their future success as a Web-based company.

Studies show that when businesses do not have a well-integrated supply chain infrastructure, they do not have the opportunity to gain all the benefits from selling online and are less able to respond to competitive innovations as they arise. Therefore, many online retailers have established their own dedicated fulfillment centers. The companies can then lower delivery costs and increase prompt action. Other organizations, which may find they are spending too much time on back-office resources, are turning toward third-party fulfillment centers. Through this approach, they can lease the skills and facilities needed for order fulfillment, rather than own their own warehouse. These fulfillment centers provide flexibility in handling large amounts of goods in short periods of time.

This is the case with the Amazon fulfillment center. Those merchants who have already been using FBA send their products to Amazon's centers. When a customer places an order with Amazon or through another merchant distribution channels, Amazon collects, packs, and ships the merchandise to the seller's customers — no matter what the time or place. FBA gives sellers the freedom to manage the order fulfillment process, while at the same time still keeping track of their inventory. With the Amazon FWS, sellers have all the FBA advantages and can incorporate FBA services right into their personal Web sites or additional sales vehicles. Inventory will then be automatically stored in Amazon's warehouses and shipped to customers when orders arrive. In short, they are establishing a virtual business. There is no cost for FWS.

However, the merchants will pay fees for goods that FBA stores and ships. The fee is based on the total per-order, per-unit, and per-pound costs. For instance, Amazon notes that the fulfillment charge for a book or CD that weighs less than a pound and sells for less than $25 would be 90 cents.

In addition, there is a 45-cents-per-cubic-foot charge for product storage, which climbs to 60 cents per cubic foot in the holiday season of October through December.

Inbound Service

With the inbound service, merchants have the opportunity to send inventory shipments to Amazon's fulfillment centers.

- **Ship products through Amazon fulfillment centers**
  With the tools available through the fulfillment centers, sellers can conveniently ship inventory to Amazon, where everything is handled, from label creation to packing slips. The seller can also take advantage of Amazon's highly discounted UPS shipping rates.

Outbound Service

The outbound service available through the fulfillment centers gives sellers the opportunity to utilize Amazon's fulfillment services for items on their Web sites or additional, non-Amazon sites.

- **Handle customer orders immediately**
  With an integration of the outbound system and the merchant software, it is possible to process customer orders in real time and immediately let Amazon know what item(s) need to be shipped and where.

- **Review and manage shipment requests**
  When orders are fulfilled, merchants can keep track of the shipment status and let buyers know when they will arrive.

- **Use personalized packing slips**
  You can also brand your packages. Amazon will place your name on the boxes, allowing customers to immediately identify the sellers.

Service Features

- **Multi-faceted**

  With FWS, merchants can easily control the numerous inbound and outbound fulfillment requests. The service offers a variety of inventory management tools, which allows the sellers to choose which orders Amazon should fulfill, and offers the flexibility to use as much or as little of the fulfillment services as they need. In addition, sellers can promote products on both their own Web sites and on Amazon; Amazon will fulfill both channels.

- **Flexible**

  Amazon FWS can alter quantity with changing customer demand, and sellers can thus ship anywhere from a few items a week to millions of orders every year. By integrating the Amazon FWS interface right into the seller's shopping cart or order management system, there is no lag time while waiting to process or batch orders. Amazon then ships products anywhere and at any time.

- **Dependable**

  With FWS, a seller's inventory is given the same quality of service as Amazon gives to its own inventory, processing millions of orders annually through complex order processing and fulfillment. With Amazon's highly efficient product searching, categorizing, and shipping system, customers know that they will be sent the product they want — when they want it.

- **Safe**

  Your inventory is safely stored in Amazon's climate-controlled inventory centers, and your buyer's orders are processed in a timely manner.

- **Assembled**

  Amazon merchants can streamline the selling process when Amazon fulfills their sales. Customer orders are processed similar to an assembly line as the system picks, packs, and ships the products. In addition, merchandise that Amazon fulfills is qualified for all of the companies' buyer shipping and customer promotions, such as free Super Saver shipping and Amazon Prime®. Plus, Amazon handles customer service and returns, which, by itself, can be very time-consuming for merchants.

CHAPTER 6

Start an Online Book Business with Amazon

When one hears the name Amazon, the word "books" immediately comes to mind, despite the fact that the company sells a lot more than it did when first coming online. It is not just new books that are for sale on Amazon. Many people rely on the ease of Marketplace to buy and sell used books as well. Or, if they are making a larger number of sales, they may want to consider Pro-Merchant. If you are a bibliophile and are always buying more books than you need, continually looking for certain books for your special collection, and/or seeking ways to make some extra money selling to others, this is an easy process. Also, if you know enough about books, then when you go to library book sales and garage sales, you will know what to pick up that other people might want.

Selling used books offers several advantages:

- They are easy to find at low cost — or even free.

- They are simple to describe and sell.

- They are easy to wrap up and ship.

- There is always a market, in good times and bad. But you will likely not make millions of dollars, however, and it takes work building this business, as with any other one. Still, you can do quite well, and if you also happen to love books, that is a bonus.

Earlier, this book covered the traits you need to work online. There are also additional personal qualities that are desirable for selling books through the Internet. You need:

- A passion for books. You need to love books and love being around them. If you are a bibliophile, no explanation is needed.

- Basic business concepts, such as organization, accounting, billing, and budgets.

- No fear of rummaging through dusty, moldy, and old boxes, attics, and basements. You will spend a great deal of time picking up books, sorting through them, cleaning them up, pricing them, putting them online, and sending them out.

- To go to flea markets, rummage sales, city dumps, and garage sales.

- An understanding that you may work a whole day and not find anything worthwhile, but then work for five minutes and find a treasure.

- A place in your home or office for piles of books that need sorting and repairs.

- To market and build your business through online opportunities. With the competition in the used book field growing all the time, sellers need to think outside of the box, continually upgrade their products, stay close to the customers' needs, and constantly watch the competition.

Also, there are some business specifics that go along with book sales. You need to establish a relationship with a local postal and shipping service. Amazon charges Marketplace book buyers a flat rate for shipping, and you receive funds to pay for the costs of packing labor and postage. The credit you receive will more often than not closely match what you pay to ship the item. Of course, you do not want to lose money on these transactions. You need to find the lowest priced, yet most efficient, service. You will also need packing supplies. Buying these wholesale either offline or online is recommended. When you consider the cost of shipping, the packing supplies must be included.

You will be spending considerable time completing and printing packaging slips. You will also be receiving and sending numerous e-mail messages. It is important for you to go with a reliable e-mail firm that will filter your spam and allow as many e-mails as necessary in your inbox. Some e-mail firms will start deleting messages after a certain amount of memory is reached; that is impractical for you. There are e-mail vendors who offer larger space and also several allowable e-mail accounts and filing systems.

It is necessary for you to set up a system that will automatically separate your incoming e-mails from Amazon, depending if they are customer requests, customer queries, or payments. With hundreds of e-mails in your inbox, you could easily lose a sale.

As you acquire more books, it will be important for you to establish an inventory system. You can use Microsoft Excel, for example. You can also go online and search for specific inventory software for booksellers. Be careful of spending too much money on this. You can easily set up your own system, as long as you are consistent and organized.

Going on a Book Hunt

Books are always easy to find, and many times, people do not realize what they are giving away. It may not be a signed first edition, but it could still be worth something to a collector. One of the obvious places to look is through local libraries.

Increasing numbers of libraries are setting up book nooks, where used books are sold on a regular basis. Sometimes, a real find can be discovered there. Public and private libraries in most towns have monthly or annual book sales. The antique book dealers may run you down for the biggest buys of library book sales, as they truly do know a book by its cover. Yet, you will not have as much competition for many of the nonfiction books, which sell better online than fiction. On the last day of the sale, you may also be able to buy many books for a few dollars, or take as much as you want free of charge. A good source for finding library sales near you is **www.booksalefinder.com**. You will also want to search such terms as "book fairs," "library sales," "books for sale," and the like for the geographical area you have designated for book searching.

If you decide to specialize, you can join antique booksellers either the night before or a few hours before the sale and pay a little bit more for a first look. As you get to know the industry, you will learn which book sales are better for specific types of books. Some libraries have more antique books, for example. But libraries are not the only places that have book sales; nonprofit organizations, schools, and civic groups often sponsor them as well.

Garage sales, tag and estate sales, and country fairs, just to name a few, are also often good sources for used books. You will not find as many as at a library sale, but the people marking the price of the books often do not understand the value of what they have. The advertisements in the paper will list books if there is a sizeable amount. If you work full-time, it is difficult to get to these sales, as they often start on Thursday or Friday morning. Sometimes, the sellers list a phone number, so you can do some sleuthing over the phone or find out if you can come early. Also find out what kinds of books are for sale. It is not worth your while to go to a sale that only has a few boxes of romance paperbacks or old encyclopedias. If you end up going to numerous estate sales, you will get to know the dealers; give them your card and let them know what you would like. If they know they are going to get a good sale by calling you, they will not wait. Also, they are always getting calls from people who are cleaning out their attics or basements. If you go to a garage sale that has interesting books for sale, remember that they do not always go quickly. Do not be afraid to make a deal, especially if you are getting several books at one time. Or, go back at the absolute end of the sale and make an offer on all the books that are left. Keep the ones you want to sell online, and give the rest to a local thrift shop or Salvation Army®.

And speaking of the Salvation Army, whenever you go into one of these stores or a church thrift shop, you will almost certainly see someone rummaging through the books. The prices are typically very low, and in addition, you could always hit the local used book stores in your area. The difficulty is the resale value. These bookstore owners know the value of their products, so there will not be any inexpensive finds. Yet, after time, you will get to know the types of books your customers want. These books may mean nothing to the bookstore, but they may be a good sale for you.

There are always auctions going on. Nonprofit organizations hold them for fundraising, and the same is true for churches and synagogues. The police, U.S. Postal Service, storage companies, and U.S. Treasury Department auctions are also good places to go hunting. Most people do not go to these auctions for the books. They are most likely looking for furniture, antiques, jewelry, and art, for example, thus you will not get trampled on by numerous dealers like you would at a library sale. Once again, it is worth calling in advance, as there are not always books at these sales. Sometimes, they never make it to the auctions, but are thrown out in advance because they are heavy and take up a lot of room.

You can even check classified ads or put one in yourself, especially if you are looking for books on a particular subject. The Bargain News and Penny Savers are much less costly than the regular dailies. Also, you can put fliers up on local bulletin boards and other places around town. Online, do not forget Craigslist^{SM} and local free classifieds or exchanges. Have a card made up with your name, address, phone number, and e-mail address, which says that you buy and sell used books. You should offer to pick up large quantities of books free of charge from anyone who is cleaning out their homes. There are always people who would gladly have you take their books away when they are spring cleaning or moving. You just need a place to sort the books and somewhere to take the books that you do not want.

What to Buy or Not to Buy

Naturally, you cannot put all the books you have online. You need to pick the juiciest ones out of the pile. You will get better at spotting these in time, especially as you become more acquainted with your buyers' interests. There are common guidelines on what books are better than others. You want to get to the point that you can find those books that can be picked up for a few dollars and sold for $25, $50, or more. Just finding a few of these each month will add considerably to total sales. In the meantime, you will start picking up books for a dollar or so and reselling them for up to $10. Here are some tips on how to do this:

- Get to know a multitude of sources for finding the value of books. In the past, you would have to purchase a new pricing guide every year as the cost would change. Now, you can get this data online. There are guides to rare and old book values, weekly resources for used book sales, online bookseller organizations, listings of book fairs, and scores of book dealers with the same book and its price.

- Do not try to sell a bestseller, unless it is still on the best-seller list. Once it goes off, it will not be worth more than any other novel. In most cases, especially because fewer books have been sold, it is better to stay with non-fiction books — unless, that is, you do your homework well and look for specific fiction books that are valuable for rarity or other reasons. In Chapter 7, more is written about textbooks, which are also sold through Amazon.

- There are, however, nonfiction books that you do not want to buy: old encyclopedias; *Reader's Digest*® magazines; the *Time-Life*ˢᴹ series; the majority of *National Geographic* magazines; most atlases; and also dated travel, reference, business, how-to, or investing books.

- A book does not have to be old to be valuable. Many out-of-print books are a find. According to BookFind-er® magazine, these were the top out-of-print books for 2008:

  - *Once a Runner (1978)* by John L. Parker, Jr.
  - *Sex (1992)* by Madonna
  - *Promise Me Tomorrow (1984)* by Nora Roberts
  - *Murmurs of Earth: The Voyager Interstellar Record (1978)* by Carl Sagan.
  - *Carpentry for Beginners: How to use tools, basic joints, workshop practice, designs for things to make (1900) by* Charles H. Hayward.

- *A Lion Called Christian (1972)* by Anthony "Ace" Bourke and John Rendall
- *Comanche Heart (1991)* by Catherine Anderson
- *Legally Sane (1972)* by Jon K. Hahn
- *Woodworker's Essential Shop Aids and Jigs; Original Devices You Can Make (1992)* by Robert Wearing.
- *The Principles of Knitting: Methods and Techniques of Hand Knitting (1989)* by June Hemmons Hiatt

Notice that some of these books are not that old. Madonna's book, *Sex*, in perfect condition and in a first edition can go for approximately $375. The book had two editions of 1.5 million each and became the most collectible coffee table book. It was also sold in other languages, which are more valuable. One avid garage sale buyer went to a bargain benefit for a local animal nonprofit fundraiser and picked up this never-opened book for $3. These are the stories that make used book-buying addictive.

There is a difference between common, limited, and rare books. Common books are listed for nearly nothing on Amazon. These are recent bestsellers and books that authored by favorite authors, such as Danielle Steel, Tom Clancy, and James Patterson. As a book seller, you should be interested in the limited category. This is where you will make most of your sales, especially as you get to know your customers' needs. These are books that are not normally found at garage sales and bookstores. These books, however, are not "rare." Look at how many Madonna books are on the market.

You should also acquaint yourself with identifying first editions. You may not readily find these, but they do exist more frequently than you might think. Look on the copyright page and see if it says "First Edition." Books printed after approximately 1965 also include a number sequence printed on the copyright page on its reprint history. A number sequence that ends at "1" such as "10 9 8 7 6 5 4 3 2 1" indicates a first printing. On the other hand, if "2" is the lowest number, as in "10 9 8 7 6 5 4 3 2," then you have a second printing. If the lowest number showing is "3," then you have a third printing. Also, check on the copyright page to see if there is a statement of a later printing, such as "Reprinted 1996" or "Second Printing." Some publishers print later editions without removing the "First Edition" statement. Books that state "First Edition" on their copyright page, but having a number sequence ending in "2" are later editions, not first editions. Of course, as with anything else, there are exceptions to the rule that you will learn as you go along.

You should set a maximum price that you are going to pay for common paperbacks, hardbacks, and textbooks. Do not go over that price unless you know a book is going for more on a "wanted" list. Normally, you will be able to buy in bulk, which lowers the price considerably. Also, purchase the books you truly want the day of a sale, then go back for the others late the next day and buy the rest.

One of the tools that you will be using when you start selling online with Amazon is the "Buyer's Waiting List." When the demand for a book is high and the supply is low, Amazon Marketplace puts it on a buyer's waiting list. On a daily basis, numerous Amazon buyers place a "pre-order" on one of these rare books, hoping that they will be able to find a copy to buy. These "waiting buyers" let the sellers know the price buyers will pay for the book, which is fortunate for sellers who might happen to have a copy stored somewhere in their house or who can locate one at a local thrift store. Nonetheless, although there are way too many books to remember, these lists offer sellers a chance to see the types of books in demand. At the top end of the Buyer's Waiting List, sellers can see a continually updated listing of the books that are most desired and see which of the more common books show a high demand.

Before the days of online information, used bookstores kept a "want list." If a customer was willing to pay a higher fee, the merchant would search in catalogs that listed rare books or telephone other book dealers in hope of locating another copy. Now, Amazon regularly updates this collectors' market. Here are examples of the top items on the list of buyers who are waiting for books:

- *Such Things Are Known* [Hardcover] by Burdick, Dorothy
  1 buyer waiting . . . **Price: $2,475**
  Minimum acceptable condition: Acceptable

- *My Second Expedition to Eastern Intertropical Africa* by Speke, John Hanning
  1 buyer waiting . . . **Price: $2,474**
  Minimum acceptable condition: Very Good

- *Sporting Incidents: Being a Collection of Sixteen Plates Done in Color*
  1 buyer waiting . . . **Price: $2,450**
  Minimum acceptable condition: Good

- *New York 1929* [Unknown Binding] by Powel, Gretchen

1 buyer waiting . . . **Price: $2,330**

Used book dealers find out that no system is infallible, and the waiting list is no different. For example, people change their minds. They may request a book and then, when it becomes available, decide they no longer want it. Or, due to a delay, that person may already have purchased it from a different source. As noted, that does not totally negate the importance of this list. It helps sellers truly get to know some of the more unique needs of their buyers. It also keeps them alert for some finds that may just come down the pike someday as they are rummaging through musty boxes of books.

There is also help available electronically. The ScoutPal, Bookhero, and ASellerTool are examples of online services that retrieve Amazon Marketplace prices and display them on a Web-enabled cell phone. These services are simple to use. You just enter the International Standard Book Number (ISBN) or Universal Product Code (UPC), and ScoutPal gathers the needed information and gives it to you in a clear form, including what is available, for how much, how many, at what sales rank, and which editions, as well as whether the book is used or new and its desirability with collectors. It is a subscription-based business, approximately $10 per month. ScoutPal and other services also offer buyer-waiting alerts on pending preorders and a means of customizing the information you need.

Expanding Your Customer Base

To increase your sales, you need to either change your prices, bring in new customers, or get more income from your present customers. You are somewhat constrained on your charges because you have to look at supply and demand. You can attract new customers and interest the old ones by offering additional information, such as a newsletter, an ongoing blog, or even a small e-book. You can also spend additional time hunting down specific groups that your veteran customers want. You should be making lists of your customers' interests and "must haves." You will need extra time to enhance your search for these customer must-haves by doing more hunting and making phone calls. You should also be setting up a network of people to call. Go on weekly trips to area thrift stores, other bookstores, and house sales. If you can increasingly fulfill more of your customers' needs, they will become loyal to you and also spread the word to others in the business. They will also turn to you whenever they want a specific book. Even if the collector has already found another copy by the time you find the desired book, you are just showing once again how you are concerned about your customers.

Grading and Describing

When you sell your books on Amazon, you will be asked about the grade or condition of the item. Some things are clearly almost black and white, with a distinct difference between them. With others, there are shades of gray, and it is difficult to know exactly where the white stops and the black starts. Grading books has this fine line of relativity, especially when there is not total agreement between booksellers. Some of the difficulties in grading books include:

- There are several different classes of books, and each has its own gradations: paperbacks, hardbacks, books with and without dust jackets, new and used books, fiction and nonfiction, and textbooks.

- What someone thinks is nothing but junk, someone else will think it is a treasure. It may be difficult to be objective all the time.

- All booksellers do not use the same terminology. They may utilize different words for the same condition, or the same word may mean something different.

Amazon stresses on its site: "An honest appraisal of the used and collectible items listed for sale at Amazon Marketplace is the first step toward ensuring a great experience for both buyer and seller." That is, every bookseller needs to do his or her best at describing the book as objectively as possible. Follow the Amazon guidelines of grading as well as you can, carefully inspect each book, look for and describe the flaws, and disclose everything you see. This is best for everyone involved. This will help ensure that the buyer has no surprises, and the seller does not get a book returned from a disgruntled customer.

Thousands of people have joined Amazon and gone into the bookselling business over the past several years. Some of them have been in the bookselling business for some time. Others are brand-new to this line of business and, as novices, are continuously learning. Grading books is something that one learns over time by seeing so many different books. It is not something that a person can learn in a brief period of time, except for glaring flaws like ripped pages or dust.

Especially on Amazon, which is so customer-centric, it is important to follow the "customer is always right" law, although it is quite difficult sometimes. This is especially true in the beginning if you are just learning the ins and outs of grading books. It is not enough to simply disclose that damage exists; you need to say where it is and how much there is. Thus, you also need to learn bookselling vocabulary, so both you and the customer will be on the same page, so to speak.

There is a lot of truth to the saying not to reinvent the wheel. If you are just starting to put books on Amazon Marketplace and are new to grading and prices, check out the price and description of the same book, which has been rated elsewhere on the site. This can give you a lot of insight into how yours should be marked. The trick with book descriptions is to be specific enough, but not too lengthy. Always honestly describe the books you have for sale. When you correctly describe your product, the buyers will be satisfied, which builds a positive reputation, loyal customers, and positive feedback comments. If you know a book is flawed, you need to add this to the comments field.

You can describe the book in 200 words. Although not used by many sellers, who are in too great of hurry to list their books, you should take advantage of this opportunity to let buyers know why you have given the specific grade of the book's condition. As explained previously, you need to familiarize yourself with the different book flaws that describe the book's condition and their abbreviations. Using Google, or another comparable search engine, the search for "book condition abbreviations" or "book condition listings" will give you a number of sites where you can get this information for free. You may also want to go to the library or purchase a book that goes into greater depth about collecting, grading, and selling books. Because you have very little space to write your description, you must be concise, clear, and honest about the condition.

Creativity is definitely acceptable — even humor, as long as there are no false promises. As noted later, expectations are key to increasing selling potential. The better the understanding of an item's condition — the good and the bad — the more the customer's expectation will be in line with what is ordered.

The Benefits of Selling Online

The Web is a perfect vehicle for selling used books, especially with many of the brick-and-mortar used bookstores closing down. You can open your online business on your own. Or, you can use services such as Amazon to help you get started and build your business. Of course, you will be paying for this service one way or another, and this is something that you will have to consider when writing your business plan. At Amazon, for example, you can sell books through Marketplace, the Advantage program, and WebStore. Future trends bode well for considering this online option.

Used book sales continue to be one of the fastest-growing categories online because the Web has made even rare books easy to find. The statistics for used books are appealing, and it requires little time to search and find a used copy of a current bestseller or a rare book that has been out of print for decades. Used book sales have increased steadily the past several years, including in the textbook category, both on and off Amazon. The economy has a great deal to do with book buying, as well, with a large jump in used book sales during questionable financial times.

CHAPTER 7

Using Amazon Marketplace to Sell Used Books

One of the best things about selling used books on Marketplace is that you do not have to shell out an insertion fee, worry about timing, or even keep track of what you have for sale. With this service, you only need to put your books online and whatever sells, sells. You will be notified whenever this happens. It is not an auction; whatever price you put on a book is what you get from the buyer. The only agreement is that you need to ship the book within two days of making the sale. This means you need to be careful with books you sell. You always want to check and see if any books have sold, even with Amazon's e-mail notice. There is always the chance that an e-mail gets lost.

If you know that you are going out of town or on vacation for a while, you should suspend sales for that time. Amazon makes it easy to temporarily stop your sales. Just click a button and everything stops until you get back. It is very important to do this because of customer ratings. You do not want people ordering books when you are unable to respond.

Further in this book, you will find information about how to join other Amazon programs. For used books, a large number of people use Marketplace. This is because of its ease and, more importantly, the millions of buyers who know that they can find their used books through Marketplace. The advertising and promotion have already been done for you.

Of course, there is a charge for selling your books on Marketplace. You pay a flat 99 cents, a commission of 15 percent of the sale, and also the variable closing fee. Amazon gives you a shipping credit to pay for sending out the product. The proceeds go directly into your account. If this worries you, you can set up a separate bank account. You set your sales price, and Amazon only collects a fee when your book sells. Amazon collects the money from your buyer, including the amount for shipping. It then deducts the commission off the sales price and the transaction fee.

> $10 for book
> + $3.49 shipping charged to buyer
> - $1.50 (15 percent commission)
> - 99 cents (cost per item)
> - $1.35 (variable closing fee, to cover refunds through A
>   to-z Guarantee program)

Amazon will waive the 99-cent transaction fee if you become an Amazon Pro-Merchant or sell in large quantity (more than 20 items per month). Only become a Pro- Merchant if you have a large number of books to sell. It will cost you $39.99 per month, but you can cancel the account at any time. As your business grows, you will know if, and when, it is applicable to move to the Pro-Merchant level.

As noted previously, Amazon Marketplace is easy to use. Registration is a standard online membership process, requesting your name, shipping and billing address, credit card information, payment method (including bank check number), birthday (optional), and e-mail address. You will want to choose a name that buyers can associate with your business. Once you feel comfortable with the selling process, you should enter your information into the "About Seller" section and include a picture or logo if you wish. In addition, you need to carefully read and accept the Participation Agreement. As usual, in order to log on, you will need to have a user ID, your name, and a password. Be sure to make a note of this password for future use. For security purposes, have the password contain both letters and numbers and more than eight characters. If you already have a personal account with Amazon, you should set up a new account here as a business. For accounting and tax purposes, it is best not to mix personal and financial and credit activities.

Once you sign on to Marketplace, you will need to click on the item detail "sell books" and enter your separate books. This can be done by using the author and title, ISBN, and/or UPC for more recent books; older books may have other codes, which you should also become familiar with. You need to make sure that you have entered the right information, such as format (hardbound or paperback, for example), date, and edition. Verify that all the information is correct.

Amazon will ask you to set a price and make recommendations. To start, you will have the opportunity to see what others are charging for the same book. You do not have to sell your book for the lowest price. Do a search online on other Web sites to determine the book's value. Also, Amazon will ask whether you want to ship internationally. Shipping internationally is excellent because it opens up many more potential customers. Be careful, as it is more expensive to ship to other countries, especially if your book is heavy. Amazon charges the customer more for international shipping; however, once in a while, that charge will not be enough money to get your book to certain countries within 14 days.

Check with the USPS for overseas' shipping rates. In some cases, such as with a paperback, it may be to your advantage to sell internationally. Many merchants do not take this option because of the extra cost. The international market is expanding significantly, and it would be worth your while to look at this option and which books may be worth your while to list for international sale.

Pricing the Book

As noted previously, it is necessary to describe the condition of each item that goes on Marketplace, and you should become familiar with the terminology involved. This is a major factor in setting the price of a book. It is also necessary because you do not want any surprises. The buyers have to know what they can expect when they open the package and see their purchase. You cannot catch everything, unless you go page by page in each book you sell; nevertheless, you should quickly look through the book to find any damage with the binding, writing inside, notes, and folded-down corners. Each seller has different guidelines for book selling. As noted previously, Amazon has its own criteria for specific items, such as computers.

- **Collectible:** Must be unique in some fashion, such as signed, rare, or out-of-print. It is important for you to explain why your copy is collectible.

- **New:** This is a book that is brand-new, never read, and in perfect condition. If it was originally plastic-wrapped, it should remain that way.

- **Like New:** This book was unread and remains in excellent condition. It has its dust cover, and there are no marks or folds on any of the pages.

- **Very Good:** This book may have been read, but it still appears to be in perfect condition. Once again, the pages have no folds or notes, and the spine is completely undamaged.

- **Good:** This book has also been read, but is also in clean condition. The dust cover is on the book and all the pages are intact, although there may be some notes and highlighting, including "from the library of" labels.

- **Acceptable:** Although this book may have a number of notes or highlighting, it is still readable. All pages are intact, but the dust cover may be missing.

- **Unacceptable:** These include books that are mildewed, stained, or unclean. They may have missing pages or text that cannot be read under highlighting. Also included are items that were used only for promotional use, such as advance reading copies (ARCs) and uncorrected proof copies.

Once you know the condition, it truly comes down to supply-and-demand and following the lead of other sellers. Unless you have a true find, you will not have to expend much effort to set the price. You need to look at the competitive offers. If you ask for much more than the average going price, you will have wait a long time to sell the book, or you may not sell it at all. Sometimes, there are bidding wars, so books are a penny. You do not want to get into this game; you will be selling books for almost nothing. Also, think about the other book dealers who are not selling their books dirt-cheap and still doing well. They sell books for a decent price that are in good-to-excellent condition and are books that sellers want. In fact, having a book at a higher price can help buyers see it as more valuable.

Textbook Sales

Most used booksellers use to shy away from textbooks, but these things have changed. A study conducted by the Government Accountability Office found that, although the price of college textbooks has not risen as much as tuition costs and other higher education expenses, it did increase twice the rate of annual inflation over the last two decades. Even though the amount spent on textbooks differs based on factors such as course load, the College Board™ reported that the cost of books and supplies for the 2005-2006 academic year ranged from $801 to $904, depending on the type of institution a student attended. This figure did not include the savings achieved by students selling their used textbooks or using financial aid. Now, given the huge increase in printed materials — about 41 percent over five years — it is becoming increasingly difficult for students to pay hundreds of dollars for these textbooks, let alone tuition and room and board. Meanwhile, the price of textbooks keeps going up.

Some books that are requested specifically by professors are difficult to buy used — particularly those that the professors have written themselves and want royalty commissions on. Colleges and universities do have different standards, however. If you can get some of these textbooks that will be used for another semester for low enough cost, in good enough condition, and recent enough for resale value, you can make yourself a nice profit.

A number of both students and parents have been using Amazon to sell used textbooks, with some books bringing better results than others — mathematics textbooks, for example. Amazon is a good place to sell these books because it is possible to reach people worldwide. Amazon attracts a lot of buyers who are specifically looking for textbooks. Here are some tips in regard to college textbooks:

- Sell your books at peak times of August, September, January and February.

- Try to resell your book as quickly as possible, as the class or the professor of the course may change requirements and replace the textbook with another.

- Research the price of your book through Amazon as well as other textbook-selling sites.

- If you plan on selling your books, do not underline or highlight text — or at least try to keep it to a minimum.

- If you smoke or eat while studying, there is a good chance that your books will offer proof. Books with sticky pages, coffee cup rings, and smoky smells do not sell well.

- Make sure the condition of your books matches the conditions that you state. If it is "used," do not list it as "like new." Also, be extremely careful of edition. Each year, another edition could become available, and students need the latest book.

- Thumb through the whole book and look for torn pages and underlined text.

- Make sure you send the exact book. Check the ISBN and binding of the book. They should match.

- Be patient and reduce your price. More often than not, you can get 40 to 50 percent of the original cost. If the book is rare, you might even get much higher than this. If there are several people selling the book on Amazon, it might be a little lower than this price.

- Try to select all shipping options when listing your book. Many sellers do not select "international shipping." If you do, you can sometimes sell your book more easily.

- Be careful about packing the book. You want people to be satisfied with what they receive from you.

Amazon now offers fulfillment services for textbook sales. The EasySell™ program ships any media items, as well as textbooks out of Amazon. The company will also store the books free for 60 days and then charge for storage. This means no more running back and forth from the post office. There is no monthly fee, but when a book sells, Amazon will charge a $1.35 variable closing fee, 99-cent set fee, and 15 percent commission on the final sale amount. If you are selling a $20 book, that will amount to $3. For students who never get around to listing the used books with any other source, it may be nice to get a few bucks every so often.

Amazon is increasing its efforts in selling textbooks through Marketplace, which is a good indication that this opportunity is growing. If you want to sell textbooks, be sure to download the "Textbook Selling Guide" on Amazon's Web site, which has best practices and frequently asked questions, and view the video for selling tips.

Other Tips for Selling Used Books

- Although Amazon will contact you each time a book is sold, it is still best to update your inventory at least every other day. You do not want to lose a sale just because you forgot to send the book out.

- If a book has not been sold in 60 days, you will receive notification. Be sure to let Amazon know your decision. If a book has been listed for 30 days without any movement, check the price and desirability with other books on Marketplace.

- Be sure to remove your listing when you are away for a vacation. Let Amazon know three to four days in advance.

- Do not rely completely on getting e-mails for sale notices. As everyone knows, e-mails can disappear into junk mail, never arrive, or get overlooked within the morass of other e-mails.

- Remember that the customer always comes first. If there is any doubt about an item, swallow your pride and give in. That person could be a big buyer next time. Also, remember Amazon's A-to-z Guarantee.

- Send e-mails letting people know when you find a book that may be of interest because of the subject. Send out other information of interest. (Ask first to make sure such e-mails are acceptable to the customer, and provide the customer with an opt-out option.)

- Include a packing slip and your business card within the shipping package.

- Respond to customer questions as soon as possible — always within 24 hours.

- Send an e-mail confirmation when you ship the book to your customer. Encourage the person to fill out a feedback form.

Dear (Name):

Thank you so much for purchasing your book from (name of company).

We received your confirmation order (date) for your Amazon.com Marketplace purchase and your (name of items) was/were shipped today through (mail service). Your shipping delivery confirmation number is (xx). You can call (telephone number) or go on (Web site) for additional information.

It can take up to (xx) business days to reach the final destination; international shipping can take up to (xx) days. If you asked for Priority Mail, it should arrive in two to three days. If you do not receive your package as expected or have any concerns when it arrives, please contact us as soon as possible (e-mail address and phone).

Comments on your buying experience can be left at **www.amazon.com/buyer-feedback**.

Thank you again for using our services. If there is any other way that (name of business) can be of help in the future, please let us know. We would be pleased to service you again with your book-buying needs.

(Your name, title)

CHAPTER 8

Publish Your Creative Works with Amazon

When people started self-publishing, their books did not have a positive reputation, and a negative stigma was attached to the concept. It was often believed that "true" authors went through regular publishing channels. But this misconception is quickly changing. According to R.R. Bowker®, in 2008, approximately 480,000 books were self-published or distributed in the United States, an increase from 375,000 in 2007. Much of this growth is from print-on-demand books. The terms self-publishing and print-on-demand (POD) publishing are increasingly becoming part of the publication lexicon. This method makes logical and financial sense. If you are not an experienced author, it is difficult — and often expensive — to get your value recognized through traditional means.

First, you need to ask yourself the real reason for publishing your book, CD, DVD, or video. Is it for gaining personal gratification, receiving public recognition, providing valuable information, promoting your business/product, or bringing in additional income? Understanding your motivation for completing the work from the very beginning will better direct your editorial and marketing efforts and give you more personal satisfaction for working toward intended goals. A brief comment about the "additional income" motivation: It is not easy to make a great deal of money from self-publishing, or publishing in general. Having your published work on an established vehicle, such as Amazon, is a good way to get visibility and promotion. Yet, it is only the very first step in marketing and sales. You have a chance to bring in some decent income if your book fits a niche that is in considerable demand, and you develop and implement a marketing plan with traditional media and online promotional tools. Just remember these "ifs." Very few authors break even on their first book.

As any established author knows, writing a book takes a strong commitment of time, dedication to following through to the end product, and a great deal of patience and persistence. Once your book is written, it is easier than ever to get it printed. There are now scores of POD service companies, such as LuLu, Xlibris®, and Outskirts Press. With these POD services, you can quickly and effectively print your book in days. Each of these book producers have different ground rules for price; number of books printed; additional services offered, such as obtaining an ISBN number; and even reviews of your book and distribution. As will be explained in greater depth in Chapter 8, Amazon also has its own POD company for books, CDs, and DVDs.

Notice that the word "print" or "produce" is used here. The "publishing" of a self-published book includes not only the production and marketing as noted, but additional steps of inventory, storage, merchandising, order processing, packing, shipping, handling returns, invoicing, and bill collecting. This is a lot of work to do on your own and is the reason why many people use a POD service, such as Amazon's. They need a way to reach the wider public and not deal with shipping out books to each customer who orders a copy through a Web site or other promotional avenue. This can be very time-consuming, especially when it is not your primary job.

Many people decide to list their book on Amazon due to the amount of traffic that the site generates for books and DVDs. By having one's published piece along with the "big guys" on Amazon, it lends credibility and also gives you a better chance of having your work seen and ordered. Using Amazon can also be an essential part of a marketing campaign. It should never be considered the entire means for sales, but it can play a part in the promotional effort. This is called a "long tail" effort, meaning that sales will come over a longer period of time. Some self-publishing authors may sell a couple thousand books over several years — or a few per month. The purpose is not to make money, but to be recognized and get your name out into the public.

CASE STUDY: BRENT SAMPSON

Brent Sampson
Outskirts Press
10940 S. Parker Rd – 515
Parker, CO 80134
888-OP-BOOKS ext. 703
www.outskirtspress.com

Brent Sampson, author of *Sell Your Book on Amazon, Self-Publishing Simplified,* and *PublishingGems: Insider Information for the Self-Publishing Writer,* is president and CEO of Outskirts Press, a successful print-on-demand publishing company with more than 2,700 titles in print as of July 2008.

When an author decides to self-publish rather than go the traditional route, he or she will find that there are numerous companies that will provide this service in addition to Amazon's CreateSpace®. Each of these PODs offers different services, and the writers should carefully compare "apples to apples," as well as weigh the differences between short-term advantages (like lower up-front costs) against long-term advantages (like lower printing costs and ongoing marketing support).

Outskirts Press, explains Sampson, "Offers the best of both worlds, by combining the advantages of independent self-publishing with the advantages of traditional book publishing." Before, during, and after publication, the author receives the support of a committed group of publishing professionals. The author receives his or her publishing rights and can set the retail price, royalty, and author discount for the book.

Sampson explains the ease of publishing with Outskirts Press in the following example:

CASE STUDY: BRENT SAMPSON

1. **Join**. Join the free author community at **www.outskirtspress.com** with just a first name and e-mail address. Receive instant access to e-books, reports, marketing advice, and industry connections.

2. **Request a rep**. Get a professional to work with you one-on-one to answer specific questions and provide suggestions to improve your book ($35 fee).

3. **Upload your book**. Submit your manuscript file online for review and publisher's evaluation for no additional cost.

4. **Select your package**. Make your package selection with recommendations based on your book.

5. **Complete information**. Customize your book with a synopsis, biography, and other personalized elements.

6. **Design, pricing, and options**. Choose your cover design, layout, and pricing plan. Set your retail price, royalty, and author discount. Elect optional upgrades and services.

7. **Upload all your files**. Submit all final copy, your author photo, and interior images, and confirm your information to approve production.

8. **Review your proofs**. Approve galley files and make any corrections.

9. **Approve for print**. Approve your final print files online and authorize publication.

10. **Publish**. Congratulations. Your book is published, and you will now begin marketing.

Book Publishing with CreateSpace® Print on Demand

If you want to print your book with a POD firm, you can find many of them listed through an online search. Or, you can use CreateSpace, which is included in the Amazon family of companies that provides total publishing, inventory and shipping, and

Internet distribution. CreateSpace works with finished manuscripts, video content, master discs, and tape formats for DVDs and CDs that are ready to be published, or a draft that requires editing, illustration, or formatting services. The company can print paperback or hardcover books. There are no setup fees or minimum orders, and you get to keep the rights to the book. CreateSpace offers an ISBN free of charge, and you are eligible to use promotional tools, such as Search Inside!™ and free shipping, and marketing materials for promotional purposes. (Please note that as of March 2008, Amazon reported that individuals who print with CreateSpace may receive more "perks" than those who use a non-affiliated POD company. Check this out when deciding on your POD vendor.)

When a customer orders your book, the royalty you earn equals the list price you set, minus CreateSpace's share. For each sale to a customer, CreateSpace calculates its share by taking a percentage of the list price, plus a fixed charge and a charge per page. The percentage of the list price varies depending on where each sale occurs. Orders you make for multiple copies of the same book shipped to a single address are called "wholesale orders" or "owner orders." For these multiple copies, you just pay the fixed charge and per-page charge, plus shipping and handling.

Each book you set up comes with the Standard Plan by default. You can upgrade to the Pro Plan at any time with a charge of $39 per book. Upgrading to CreateSpace's Pro Plan reduces the fixed and per-page charges for these orders; the company does not offer discounts based on volume. You pay for these when placing your order, and you do not earn royalties when buying copies. You are charged sales tax on certain orders unless CreateSpace has a valid resale certificate from you when ordering. The cost for a proof copy is the same as the cost for a single book order. You pay this amount when you place your order, and you do not earn royalties for proof copies. You can make your title available to millions of customers by selling on CreateSpace eStore, Amazon, and on your own Web site.

Selling Through the CreateSpace eStore

A CreateSpace eStore is a free, customizable sales page that allows you to sell directly to customers. Although it is hosted on **www.CreateSpace.com**, and your domain will be under the CreateSpace address, you can tailor the Web site to have the same look as your own site, so buyers have a seamless sales experience. Many CreateSpace members use their eStores specifically for driving customer traffic to their product line. You can have a separate eStore for each of your titles published. It has a customizable banner and description; promotional clips, so customers can see a portion of your work before ordering it; and tailored background and text color. You can even upload a QuickTime™ movie or a Windows Media® file. You will have access to a report with customer information for monthly sales made through your eStore along with your royalty payment. You can also receive this information in daily or weekly e-mails, if you prefer. CreateSpace charges shipping and handling fees directly to your customers, so payment does not affect the amount of money you receive for each sale. Similarly, CreateSpace handles returns and other customer service issues via e-mail.

Selling Through Amazon

Amazon's retail program allows you to make your book, CD, or DVD title available for sale to its millions of customers. Amazon's program differs from the one for CreateSpace eStore in the way customer traffic is directed toward your title. With the CreateSpace eStore, you are essentially driving traffic to your title. On the other hand, with the Amazon retail program, you are directing interested Amazon customers to your book, DVD, or CD product page via a variety of features such as, "Search," "Browse," and "Recommendations." In order to participate with the Amazon retail program when adding a new title in your member account, enable "Amazon Retail" under "Sales & Promotion" or the default selection for new titles. Amazon and CreateSpace will then work together to build a free title detail page on the Amazon Web site. To alter the retail settings for your title, click on the edit icon, the pencil, next to the title you would like to edit. Then, click on the "Edit" link next to the "Sales & Promotion" section, and you will be able to modify the Amazon settings. After putting your title up for sale, it may take as long as 15 business days for the initial Amazon listing to be active. Sales made through the Amazon retail program appear on the online member reports and e-mailed sales reports. Amazon assumes responsibility for customer service, shipping, and returns. Customers buying products that are $25.00 and above are eligible for free Super Saver Shipping.

Costs for Publishing

Our share - percentage of list price	
CreateSpace eStore	20% of list price per sale
Amazon.com	40% of list price per sale

Charges for black & white books All trim sizes	Standard	☆ Pro Plan
Books with 24 - 108 pages Fixed Charge	$3.66 per book	$2.15 per book
Charge per Page	None	None
Books with 110 - 828 pages Fixed Charge	$1.50 per book	$0.85 per book
Charge per Page	+ $0.02 per page	+ $0.012 per page

Charges for color books All trim sizes	Standard	☆ Pro Plan
Books with 24 - 40 pages Fixed Charge	$6.55 per book	$3.65 per book
Charge per Page	None	None
Books with 42 - 250 pages Fixed Charge	$1.75 per book	$0.85 per book
Charge per Page	+ $0.12 per page	+ $0.07 per page

An **amazon**.com. company

Royalty Example

Winter Snows is a black-and-white book with 150 pages of short stories. The author set the list price as $16. The chart below shows how the royalty is calculated for sales with CreateSpace Standard Plan and with Amazon.

	eStore Sale	Amazon.com Sale
List Price set by you	$16.00	$16.00
- Our Share	$7.70	$10.90
Your Royalty	**$8.30**	**$5.10**

CreateSpace Share Details

	eStore Sale	Amazon.com Sale
Percent of List Price	$ 3.20 20% of $16.00	$6.40 40% of $16.00
Fixed Charge	$1.50	$1.50
Charge per Page 150 pages at $0.02 per page	$3.00	$3.00
Fixed Charge	$1.50	$1.50
CreateSpace Share Total	$7.70	$10.90

An **amazon**.com. company

Standard versus Pro E-Store Example

Go back to the example book, *Winter Snows*. The below chart shows the royalty earned for each sale of this book under the different plans:

	Standard Plan		☆Pro Plan	
	E-Store	Amazon.com	E-Store	Amazon.com
List Price	$16.00	$16.00	$16.00	$16.00
CreateSpace Share	$7.70	$10.90	$5.85	$9.05
Royalty	**$8.30**	**$5.10**	**$10.15**	**$6.95**

An **amazon**.com. company

DVD Publishing with CreateSpace POD

CreateSpace, with its DVD-on-Demand service, takes your master disc and duplicates it for sale on Amazon. It can accommodate multi-disc cases, with up to four discs in one case. Once your disc is ready to send in, burn a copy and mail it to CreateSpace. It will prepare a proof copy with final printing and packaging for your review and approval before your titles goes live. If you are authoring your own DVD, there are several submission requirements:

- **Bit rate:** The maximum total bit rate for the video and audio tracks needs to be 6.5 megabits per second (mbps), which optimizes playback compatibility on older players and computers.

- **Audio:** Dolby Digital (AC-3) audio needs to be used, not MPEG audio, as DVD players purchased in the United States are not guaranteed to have MPEG audio decoders. Also, any title with MPEG audio could actually play silently on some playback units.

- **File size:** The DVD-R cannot be larger than a file size of 4.7 billion bytes, and the original copies need to be single-sided, single-layer discs.

- **Test your disc:** CreateSpace is not responsible for any glitches in the discs it receives. They print as-is. If any problems are in the source copy, these will occur in the copies, as well. Also, the sources need to be tested in three or more different models of set-top DVD players.

- **File system format:** The source copy must only include the Audio TS and Video TS folders. Other files could lead to compatibility problems and playback issues on certain DVD players. CreateSpace does support data inclusion or executable files on DVDs.

Royalty for DVDs

Amount earned on sales = Your list price minus CreateSpace share (shown below)	
CreateSpace's Share	
Fixed Charge	**$4.95 / unit***
Share for sales On E-Store	**+15% / sale**
Share for sales on Amazon.com	**+45% / sale**

An **amazon**.com. company

DVD Duplication Orders

quantity	Price / unit*
1-49	$4.95
50-99	$3.96
100-500	$2.97
500+	Contact CreateSpace for orders over 500

An **amazon**.com. company

Video Publishing with CreateSpace POD

If you want CreateSpace to handle your DVD authoring, you can send your videotape(s), a menu image, and some general information. Do not send the master — only a high-quality duplication.

Your source material will be stored in the Future Proof Archive for security purposes and to make it easier to release in various future formats. CreateSpace can accept your video in the following formats:

- BetaCam® SP (BetaSP)
- Mini DV
- VCAM®
- DVC™ Pro (not 50)
- Digital BetaCam (DigiBeta)
- VHS (not recommended)
- BetaCam SX
- MPEG IMX®

- 1" (1-inch) D2
- S-VHS
- U-Matic® (3/4")

Do not use the long-playing mode. All tapes must be in National Television System Committee (NTSC) format along with a time code. If you cannot produce a copy in one of these formats, a local video production shop will be able to help you.

Both the tape and case need a label with the six-digit Title ID. Mark the tape number with multiple tapes, for example "Title 123456 Tape 1/3." The tape must begin and end with at least 20 seconds of leader with a time code. Check over the duplicate to make sure audio levels are correct, with high points never exceeding 0db. Too much volume can cause considerable quality loss, particularly when digitally encoded; CreateSpace receives many tapes with this problem.

Royalty for Videos

You can download videos through Amazon's Unbox™, an option when you join CreateSpace. Customers are able to buy and rent top-quality videos from the Amazon Web site and download them to any Windows-compatible computer that has the Unbox video player installed. Certain TiVo℠ subscribers can also purchase and download these videos. You may offer one of your titles by using Unbox, DVD-on-Demand, or both simultaneously. Customers can purchase a "Download-to-Own" title, which they can watch unlimited times. Or, they can choose the "Download-to-Rent" option and watch the video for a limited period of time. From each sale, you get a 50 percent royalty minus any taxes, shipping and handling, returns, specials, and credits when Unbox customers rent or purchase any of your videos for sale. For instance, if you had a video that was Downloaded to Own for $14.99, you would receive $7.49. On the other hand, if your video was Downloaded to Rent for $3.99, you would make $1.99.

Music Publishing with CreateSpace POD

You can also use CreateSpace if you want Amazon customers to hear the music you composed and/or sang or played. Those visiting Amazon MP3 can listen to samples, buy individual tracks or whole albums, and download samples on their MP3 player or computer. CreateSpace members have the opportunity to sell through Amazon MP3, CreateSpace Audio CD-on-Demand, or the two simultaneously. When your product is placed on either Audio CD- on-Demand or Amazon MP3, both options are a single cost. This is done by using the "Audio Download" option to add a title, or the "Amazon MP3" option for an existing title. If you decide to use the Amazon MP3 sales channel, you cannot include any advertisements within your audio tracks/files. As a CreateSpace participant, you earn a royalty when Amazon MP3 customers buy a track(s) from your album or entire album. The number of tracks on the album determines your album royalty.

You must submit your music only on CD-R or replicated CD. Keep your master and send a duplicate. You cannot have more than 72 minutes (700MB), which meets the Red Book Audio CD standard. The following information describes the exact parameters and properties of an Audio CD: 1) Digital audio encoding with 2-channel signed 16-bit PCM sampled at 44100 Hz. 2) Using the Audio CD option in burning software to automatically produce an audio CD that meets specifications. CreateSpace also will not accept data CDs with audio files, such as MP3 and wav. Only those with tracks conforming to the Red Book standards are acceptable. The CD disc must have the seven-digit Title ID put directly on the face and case with a permanent marker. As is always the case, it is necessary to carefully and completely test your CD on a number of different CD players before sending it to CreateSpace. If there are any problems on this disc, each unit made will have the sample problems.

MP3 Royalty

Royalties are earned when customers buy a track(s) on the album or when they buy the whole album. The Amazon MP3 sales report in your Member Account is updated monthly, and your payment for sales occurs in 60 days following the end of the month when the item was sold.

Audio Download Royalty Calculation		
Number of Album Tracks	Royalty per Track Sale	Royalty per Album Sale
10 or more	$0.65	$6.18
9 tracks	$0.65	$5.81
8 tracks	$0.65	$5.17
7 tracks	$0.65	$4.52
6 tracks	$0.65	$3.88
5 tracks	$0.65	$3.23
4 tracks	$0.65	$2.58
3 tracks	$0.65	$1.94
2 tracks	$0.65	$1.29
1 tracks	$0.65	$0.65

An **amazon**.com. company

CASE STUDY: MICHELLE L. LONG, CPA, MBA

Michelle L. Long, SPA, MBA
Long for Success, LLC
Lee's Summit, MO
Phone: 816-524-7799
www.longforsuccess.com

Michelle Long realized she had the experience and skill needed to publish her own book, given her background as a CPA, owner of M. Long Consulting. She has an MBA in entrepreneurship and has been an adjunct teacher of strategic management at the University of Missouri, Kansas City, as well as a QuickBooks consultant and coach.

As a result, she became one of the first authors to use Amazon's CreateSpace for self-publishing. Her book, *Successful QuickBooks Consulting,* has proved successful, too, with approximately 3,000 sold within two years. "It's great. Now that the book is listed on Amazon and my own Web site, I don't have to do anything but watch the money be direct deposited into my bank account." Amazon handles the printing, mailing, and invoicing. She has also been pleased with CreateSpace's quality and customer service.

Appropriately, Long has not solely relied on Amazon's marketing and promotion vehicles for pushing her book. She uses the signature, "Author of…" in all her mailings and comments on forums that are directly related to her book's topic. "I give advice on the forums, rather than a hard sell, but they see my signature, and many may follow up and order the book," Long said. She's also promoting it through industry conferences and newsletters. "If you don't market," she said, "you will not sell."

CASE STUDY: MICHELLE L. LONG, CPA, MBA

Through Amazon's sales data, which is available through CreateSpace, Long can see that her best sales days are Tuesday, Wednesday, and Thursday, so these are the optimal days for posting on forums. She also has the first chapter of her book downloadable for free from her Web site. Long plans on writing additional books on Quick-Books, as this has been such a successful niche.

The Amazon system keeps Long's sales growing: The better the book is in the rankings, the more it is displayed and recommended. This leads to more sales and a better ranking, and the cycle keeps going.

CHAPTER 9

Using Amazon Advantage for Creative Sales

In the previous chapter, you learned about self-publishing a book, CD, or DVD. Now, how can you promote the work once it is completed? This is where the Advantage Program will help you sell the book you just wrote, the CD your band just completed, or the video you are offering for training purposes. A growing number of people are recognizing the value of selling information for both expertise and entertainment through self-published books, e-books, videos, CDs, DVDs, and now, electronic books for Amazon's Kindle. Amazon also accepts enrollment of software, video games, PC game titles, and vinyl records into the Advantage program, in addition to books.

Finding an established publisher and marketer for your work is becoming increasingly difficult, as publishers merge and spend more of their resources on established authors and expected best-sellers. Getting established is one way that the Amazon Advantage Program can help. The Advantage Program is particularly helpful for introducing new works to the market. Titles that are a part of Advantage qualify for Amazon's fulfillment support, promotional assistance, and shipping specials. On the contrary, Marketplace transactions occur directly between you and the customer. You need to list the item, handle shipping, and provide all customer service. Amazon only handles payment processing for the transactions.

Amazon Advantage Program Highlights

The following is a list of benefits that Advantage provides:

- When becoming an Advantage member, Amazon keeps several of your books in the warehouse ready for packaging, shipping, and invoicing. CDs and videos are also in stock and ready to be mailed. Because Amazon shows these "in stock" books first and more frequently to buyers, customers are more likely to notice and buy them.

- Amazon shows specialized, niche, or hard-to-find items to potential buying customers who are most likely to purchase them. The company's technology "knows" the buyers' interests and helps them see items they did not know existed. Merchandise shown is based on the customers' browsing and buying history, such as with the "Customers who bought this... also bought this" feature.

- Your book can be marketed in a number of different ways on Amazon, which will be covered in more depth in Chapter 10. These include "Search Inside!," customer reviews, community interaction, and author biographies.

- You are able to manage your entire business with the Advantage Web site all day and night each and every day. You can stock a quantity of up to five of your items in the Amazon's distribution center, and your titles are listed for immediate availability on Amazon. When you have a sale, Amazon will send you an e-mail and ask you to send more inventory if necessary.

- Amazon retains ownership of customer returned items and stores them as part of company-owned inventory.

- You get paid right at the end of each month after the month of sale without invoicing. If a book sells in April, you will receive payment for it at the end of May through electronic funds transferred to your bank, or by check.

"With the Amazon Advantage Program, the customer sets the list price for the merchandise. Yet, Amazon reserves the right to set the retail price to customers at its sole discretion. It can decide to discount products based on a number of considerations that vary over time. Amazon offers discounts on hundreds of thousands of selected titles every day and cannot confirm when, if ever, a title will be discounted or how long a title will remain at any particular discount."
— *From the Amazon Web site.*

amazon.com

Amazon, Amazon.com and the Amazon.com logo are registered trademarks of Amazon.com, Inc. or its affiliates.

Amazon Advantage Program Requirements

All Amazon Advantage Program books, CDs, DVDs, and videos must have a publishing code to be accepted. Books are printed with the ISBN, which delineates the book title and its variety of book formats, including multiple editions, hardcover, paperback, audiocassette, and CD-ROM. The POD printer, for an extra cost, will help the customer apply for the ISBN. You will normally have everything in approximately three to five weeks. If you are not from the United States, request information about ISBN registry for your country. Additional information and application can also be received from:

International Standard Book Numbering Agency
www.isbn.org
R.R. Bowker
121 Chanlon Road
New Providence, NJ 07974
Phone: 877-310-7333

Instead of an ISBN, music CDs, DVDs, and videos have a UPC. A UPC has 12 digits. The first six digits identify the company. The next five digits delineate the specific product. The last digit checks for accuracy. Additional information and applications can be received from:

GS1 US, INC.
www.gs1us.org
8163 Old Yankee Road, Suite J
Dayton, OH 45458 USA
Phone: (937) 435-3870

EANS stands for European article number, and is primarily used in Europe and the United Kingdom for music CDs, DVDs, and videos.

All books listed with the Advantage Program must also have a barcode, which is a symbol that can be optically scanned for title, ISBN/UPC, and price. The barcodes on your products determine how quickly Amazon shipments are received into inventory and available to customers for sale. The complete name for the barcode format is Bookland® EAN Barcode with 5-digit Add-on Code (or Price Code). The ISBN is printed above the barcode and the Bookland EAN code is below. The first three digits tell the scanner that the item is a book or a book-related product. Then come the first nine digits of the ISBN and a check digit to verify that the scanner has correctly read the barcode.

CDs, videos, and DVDs must have the UPC code instead of the ISBN, which can also be translated into a barcode format. The first digit is the prefix for the Uniform Code Council (UCC), the organization that administers the UPC and other retail standards. With only a few exceptions, the next five numbers are the UCC company prefix, and the final five numbers identify the specific product. At the end is a check digit, which allows the scanner to verify that the item has scanned properly. The UPC-A barcode, also known as a "UCC-12," has a total of 12 digits.

Ideally, barcodes should be integrated into the design of the product. If your merchandise has already been manufactured or printed, barcode labels can be produced after printing and applied to the outer packaging or cover. Anyone who supplies an item with a barcode to Amazon must ensure that it complies with the following guidelines:

- Amazon must be able to scan the barcode, so there can be nothing, such as outer packaging, to obscure the view. The barcode has to be located on the back of the product, in the lower right quadrant. It is mandatory to shrink-wrap CDs and DVDs in order to protect them during shipping and to distinguish them from used items. The barcode must be seen through the packaging in order to properly scan.

- The barcode must scan to the original ISBN or UPC number.

- The owner of the product needs to test the barcode with a certified verifier in order to ensure the parameters that contribute to a high-grade barcode. A barcode scanned by the local bookstore is not equivalent to having it verified. If you print your own barcodes, make sure that this process did not create any defects that reduce barcode performance.

- The barcode should be printed with black ink on a white background with a 1/4-inch of white space on the left and right side. This is known as the "quiet zone."

- If an item has both an ISBN and a UPC, Amazon requires that it be listed only under its UPC.

- Amazon recommends the following as vendors for questions regarding and the production of barcodes:

FineLine Technologies
www.finelinetech.com
157 Technology Parkway, Suite 700
Norcross, GA 30092
Phone: (800) 500-8687
Fax: (678) 969-9201

AccuGraphiX
www.bar-code.com
3588 E Enterprise Drive
Anaheim, CA 92807-1627
Phone: (800) 872-9977
Fax: (714) 630-6581

Fotel Inc.
www.fotel.com
1125 E. St. Charles Road, Suite 100
Lombard, IL 60148
Phone: (800) 834-4920
Fax (630) 932-7610

Eversio Technologies
www.eversio.com
844 NW 49th
Seattle, WA 98107
Phone: (888) 333-9001
Fax: (206) 284-0915

As noted, before registering for Advantage, you need to have an
ISBN or UPC number and a scannable barcode that matches this
ISBN. You also need to have your book, video, or CD printed in

a small quantity. You can do this through Amazon's own POD or one of the many other similar organizations. At this point, you do not need any more than a dozen copies: some for your own use and others to send to Amazon for approval.

Amazon Advantage Sign-Up

Go to the Amazon Web site and click on Advantage at the bottom. After you put in your name and password, Amazon will ask you to accept the program agreement and then request general information required for enrollment on your contacts and banking specifics. You will hear back within five days regarding approval.

Becoming a member of Amazon Advantage is not costly. Yet, you may be surprised about the consignment fee. In the bookselling business, the authors do not normally get a high percentage of the fee unless they market and sell the book themselves. In this case, Amazon charges an annual fee of $29.95 for membership to Advantage. This includes unlimited title enrollment. The standard commission rate is 55 percent, where 45 percent of the list price goes to you and 55 percent of each unit sold goes to Amazon. As noted previously, you decide on the price at which it will be listed, or the "suggested retail price," but Amazon can lower the price of the item under the list price; in this case, Amazon pays from its percentage. For instance, if the suggested retail price is $39.95, you get $17.98 when selling a copy, even if the price is later discounted.

CHAPTER 10

Advantage Marketing and Promotional Tools

Because Amazon makes a large portion of its annual income from selling books and other published materials, the company offers a number of different ways that authors can market their books to customers. Spend a few minutes traveling around the Amazon Web site, and you will quickly see examples of the promotional vehicles.

With the rationale behind the "Search Inside!" feature on Amazon, you can allow customers to preview the content of your book. The potential customer must either have purchased something from Amazon previously or needs to register in order to use this feature. "See Sample Pages" takes readers to different sections of the book, such as the cover, index, or contents page; "Surprise Me" gives them an excerpt from the book. "Search Inside!" gives the customer the chance to see all the listings of the searched word and read those specific pages. Advantage vendors are automatically approved for "Search Inside."

> "The unit growth for the titles enrolled in this program [Search Inside!] usually outpaces those that aren't in the program by several percentage points, so we encourage authors and publishers to enroll." — *From the Amazon.com Web site.*

amazon.com

Amazon, Amazon.com and the Amazon.com logo are registered trademarks of Amazon.com, Inc. or its affiliates.

Since its introduction of the Kindle reader, Amazon has placed more of an emphasis on digital books. The "Upgrade" program not only lets customers view sections of the book through the search mode, but also the whole book online if they decide to order it. While they are waiting for their book to arrive in the mail, they can read it via Amazon's Web Services. Sometimes, Amazon may include additional materials other than the book; with literature classics, for example, the reader may get a CliffsNotes™ study guide.

Building community is a common theme when discussing Amazon and promotional tools in general. Amazon has a following of millions of dedicated buyers who respect and laud Amazon for its customer service. This is the community in which you want to establish yourself. The first thing that you will do as an author is to sign-up for AmazonConnect®, where you will include your biography and any other information you have included, such as Listmania℠ and "So You'd Like To…Guide."

AmazonConnect also gives authors the online ability to post messages directly to their own product detail pages and individual Amazon blogs. It showcases the three most recent posts by the author/artist. Amazon also features an AmazonConnect Directory, where authors are listed alphabetically and readers can find the detail pages of their favorite artists. This is an effective way for you to increase readership by building a better relationship with your community of readers.

When you create your profile page, any customer information associated with your existing account will be available, including reviews, wish lists, and registries. If you already have a blog outside of Amazon, you can use Really Simple Syndication (RSS) to connect your existing blog directly to your Amazon customers. In your profile, you will be mentioning your books and other information that promotes you as an expert. You should also add a photo of yourself and/or any other images that depict your interests or geography. This profile is very important because it will be on all the pages where you comments are included. Below is a sample of Steve Weber's profile.

Steve Weber, author of "Plug Your Book!"

New Reviewer Rank: 6,830 (?)
Classic Reviewer Rank: 26,587

Helpful votes received on all contributions: 88% (647 of 741)

Location: Northern Virginia, USA

E-mail: feedback@weberbooks.com

Web Page:
http://www.weberbooks.com/se...

Biography:
Steve Weber, one of the most successful self-publishing writers on Amazon.com, is the author of "ePublish: Self-Publish Fast and Profitably for Kindle, iPhone, CreateSpace and Print on Demand."

Steve's "Plug Your Book!" teaches authors how to promote themselves using Internet social networking.

Steve's other title, "The Home-Based Bookstore," explains how entrepreneurs can start an online book r... Read more

amazon.com

Weber's *Plug Your Book* is all about such opportunities. He covers the many different ways to market your book to your specific targeted customers. Says Weber:

"Word-of-mouth is the only thing that can make a book really successful. And this has always been the challenge: How can the author break through? Until recently, it usually required 'pull' – connections with powerful allies in the publishing food chain. Today, creative writers can connect with readers directly. The only requirements are a link to the Internet and the will to plug in. Now, for the first time, authors and readers can ignite word-of-mouth using online communities to spread the word about good books. Anyone with the skills to write an e-mail can publicize a book worldwide effectively and economically."

Other information that can be added to your author profile are your reviews of different books or products. These consist of the one-to-five star rating that summarizes everyone's feedback. Reviews that are helpful rise to the top of the list. In addition, the "Listmania" list shows how you, personally, would categorize items based on a specific theme. You can use this tool to promote your book by choosing merchandise that will interest your target audience or individuals who are interested in your topic or want more information. It will not only appear on the page with your book, but with any other book that is on your list. It considerably adds to your exposure, especially if you have a lengthy list of books. You will want to continually update your lists with the most popular books listed.

Make sure that the title of your list specifically lets the potential customers know exactly what the list will entail: for example, "How to Start an Online Business: Perfect for the Novice." Your product will be among those listed, but not necessarily first. There may be books by more known authors or higher sellers. Right after the headline, you will be able to write a very brief comment. This comment should provide the reason why you are an expert in this field and why these books are worth reading. It should motivate them to look closely at what is listed. For example, "E-commerce is growing like wildfire, but successful online merchants understand the medium and how to gain the greatest benefit. These books will provide that foundation you need before taking that first big step." You will also be making short comments on each of the books, including your own book. Customers can vote on the helpfulness of your book, and Amazon shows how many people have viewed your list. The better you do on the rating and readership, the more people will see your book.

A similar opportunity that Amazon offers are "So You'd Like to…Guides" Using the same example as above, you could have a "So you'd like to start a successful online business." A Guide is a much more comprehensive and informative vehicle than Listmania. Rather than just listing books, you will be commenting about these books and the topic they are addressing. For example, you may have a list of books about whether or not an online business is right for you. Should you quit your current career and jump into e-commerce? Your Amazon Guide will discuss some of the issues involved with this, some of the books written, and other Web sites that may be of interest. You will want to write a number of different guides, as this will build your image as an expert and increase exposure. Be sure to provide solid, knowledgeable information. Fluff or cut-and-pasted information from something else that has been written is unacceptable. You also want to make sure that your author profile, which shows your area of expertise, is relevant to this topic.

Because you are an expert, you should also be writing reviews of other books in your field. This takes time because you are not going to review a book that you have not actually read. Also, one-liners will not do. You want to have at least 150 words that provide insight into the book. Your review will include your "signature," which is a brief overview of your expertise, such as "... author of ... (your book)." The more reviews you write, the more exposure you will receive. In the book *Sell Your Book on Amazon*, author and case study participant Brent Sampson recommends 100 reviews, just as a starting point.

Another way for authors to increase their customer base is to promote their shorter works, allowing readers to get a feel for style and theme. Many authors write in shorter literary form in addition to full-length books. "Amazon Shorts" sells previously unpublished, short-form literature. Your fiction and nonfiction pieces on just about any topic in a digital format sell for $.49, either as a PDF download or on Kindle. This is a productive way to keep in touch with your readers on a frequent basis. All Advantage authors are eligible to submit work to this program, but it is not available at all times.

Amazon also gives a couple of options for paid advertising for merchandising purposes. Personalization is a very well-known aspect of Amazon. When a customer logs in to the Amazon homepage, he or she is immediately greeted with works that may be of interest based on prior buying history. When requesting a specific book or book subject, Amazon recommends other possible products to consider. One of the programs built on this concept is "The Buy X, Get Y (BXGY) Program" or the Amazon co-op, which gives you the opportunity to feature your work in the "Best Value" or "Better Together®" part of a different product's detail page.

In this promotional tool, your book is paired with a similar theme or subject matter of another work on Amazon, even a bestseller. They are advertised on that book's page with a direct link to your title and an additional 5 percent discount.

Frequently Bought Together

Price For Both: $33.34

[Add both to Cart]   [Add both to Wish List]

Show availability and shipping details

☑ **This item:** The Waiter & Waitress and Wait Staff Training Handbook: A Complete Guide to the Proper Steps in Service for Food & Beverage Employees by Lora Arduser

☑ The Food Service Professionals Guide To: Waiter & Waitress Training: How To Develop Your Wait Staff For Maximum Service & Profit (The Food Service Professionals Guide, 10) by Lora Arduser

amazon.com

Amazon, Amazon.com and the Amazon.com logo are registered trademarks of Amazon.com, Inc. or its affiliates.

Advantages and Disadvantages of "Better Together"

Thumbs Up

- **Helping to increase the number of books sold.** Consumer research shows that promotional programs like this leverage the fact that consumers like to save money, and people who look for a specific product are more apt to buy an additional complementary product if it is easily accessible.

- **Building image.** Readers want to purchase books from authors who are experts in their field. This advertising program offers the prestige of pairing your book with a top seller from Amazon, if you pay the higher price of $750 a month.

- **Gaining additional exposure on Amazon.** The more times your potential customers see your book, the better. With "Better Together," a book essentially doubles its chances of being noticed by potential buyers.

Thumbs Down

- **Shelling out a lot of money.** Spending $500 or $750 for one month to pair with another title is a high price to pay for most self-published authors — and it takes many sales to recoup the investment.

- **Pairing may be difficult.** It is often a challenge to get your book paired with a bestseller because of all the other writers who want to couple with the same book.

- **Coupling with the right book**. The other book with which you pair must be similar enough in theme that the readers will want to take the gamble on yours.

Ways to Increase Amazon Advantage Sales

- Enhance the possibility of receiving positive reviews. As soon as you are published, send your work to your colleagues, peers, family members, and friends and ask them to send an honest, yet (you hope) favorable, review to Amazon. If you receive a positive comment to your Web site or blog, forward it on to Amazon. If you receive positive reviews in print media, including your local papers, request that these be sent to Amazon.

- Whenever you write a comment on a blog or forum, leave a signature with a link to your latest book at Amazon.

- Become an Associate and put a link on your Web site or blog, allowing visitors to order the book.

- Under the name of the title of your book on Amazon is a "Share Your Own Customer Images." Download several photos that are theme-connected.

- Make sure that your profile is up-to-date and then complete Listmania, reviews, "So You'd Like To...," Guides, and other community comments.

- Sign up with AmazonConnect and connect your blog to Amazon, and vice versa.

- Make sure that you sign up for "Search Inside!" for your book.

- Have the electronic form of your book put on Kindle.

- Pay for the "Better Together" Amazon promotion.

- When your next book is published, send a note about it to the previous book's buyers. More than 65 percent of books are bought by returning customers.

CHAPTER 11

Affiliate Marketing 101

D epending on the version of history told, Amazon's CEO Jeff Bezos was either the first, or one of the first, to develop the affiliate concept. One night, shortly after he started his new online business, Bezos was talking with a woman at a cocktail party about how she wanted to sell books on her Web site. He thought about the conversation and came up with the idea of linking the woman's site to Amazon and giving her a commission on any book sales. It was through Amazon that the affiliate program became so widespread online.

The affiliate program has been of major benefit to online retailers ever since. As the Internet has continued its expansion, and growing numbers of worldwide consumers have gone online for their purchases, retailers have looked for a myriad of ways to grow their business, expand their name brand, and acquire new customers. Affiliate marketing, or known as the "Associate Program" on Amazon, has been this company's thoroughbred race horse since the concept first began. In a short period of time, through its Associate Program, the company was able to spread its brand across thousands of Web sites. In February 1998, Amazon had already attracted more than 30,000 Associates in place of a minimal commission on sales. Now, that number stands at approximately one million.

Becoming an Associate with Amazon gives a business the opportunity to team up with one of the largest online retail companies with a very well-known brand name. It is an excellent way to drive people to a Web site and to offer additional product beyond what you are already selling. The search engines follow affiliates and will give them a good ranking. There is no cost for additional inventory. Amazon supplies the shopping cart, processes the orders and payments, ships the products, and handles returns. You get a commission on anything sold.

In brief, Internet merchants want additional business either in leads or sales, and they know they have to pay for them. With the affiliate network, both the merchant and the new Web site partners benefit. The merchant gets the additional business. In return, the affiliates have an opportunity to play a role in a much larger production. They do not need to invest a lot of money. They only need a very basic knowledge of Web site production, an interested in a specific product or service, and a basic understanding of the Internet.

Affiliates are independent online entities that agree to provide links to a merchant's Web site. In this arrangement, affiliates receive a sales commission, percentage of each sale, and/or click-through to the merchant's Web site. When affiliates sign up with a merchant, they get special links that are coded with a unique account number. These links are then placed on banner advertisements, buttons, text, or even turn-key stores on the affiliate's Web page. The affiliates upload the Web pages to their server. When visitors click on a link, special software records the coded transaction.

If a visitor makes a purchase or fulfills a lead as a result of a referral, the affiliate's account is credited with the appropriate amount. Payment terms vary from program to program. Cookies in affiliate marketing are used for persistently determining the affiliate's entitlement to commission over a particular range of time. The cookie lifetime tracks the period of time that a cookie stays valid on a user's personal computer. Given a set lifetime of 30 days, for example, the affiliate is allowed a commission for all leads and sales that take place up to 30 days after the customer's initial click on the advertising link. Most merchants pay their affiliates monthly or quarterly once the affiliate has reached a predetermined balance in the account. Merchants provide affiliate account information via e-mail or private Web sites. Affiliate marketing can provide a steady flow of income based on impressions (how many visitors see the offer); click-throughs (the number of visitors who click on the offer); and leads/sales (the total of visitors who make a purchase and how much is made from each sale). The amount of traffic a Web site generates, or the number of visitors, is of utmost importance.

With affiliate marketing, important measurements include:

- **Unique visitor count:** Every time someone comes to the site, the IP addresses are recorded, which counts the total number of people who have come to the Web site. If, for example, someone visits 20 pages within a

Web site, the server will count just a single visitor (since the page accesses are all part of the larger IP address), but 20 page accesses. Unique visitor count is calculated by totaling the number of different clients who access the server.

- **Click-through rate (CTR):** This is the amount of clicks your ad receives divided by how many times your ad is shown (impressions). It is expressed as a percentage. You need to recognize the difference between what the click-through rate will and will not measure. You will know the percentage of visitors who clicked on the ad to get to your destination site; however, you will not know those who did not click, but went to the site later because they saw the advertisement. Thus, the CTR can be thought of as measuring the immediate reaction to an ad, but not the overall response.

- **Conversion rate:** This is the percentage of people who respond in the way desired. This desired action can take a variety of avenues. Examples include product sales, membership registration, newsletter or e-zine subscriptions, software downloads, or other activities other than mere page browsing. The conversion rate you get will be based on two major factors that must work properly to bring the wanted results: how much the person is interested and attracted to the offer, and how easy it is to complete the process. The person's degree of interest is increased by pairing the right individual, place, and time. The degree of interest includes the value of what is offered and its presentation. Usually, minor items one buys on impulse will covert better than something that is costly. The ease in which the action is completed is based on the usability of the site, navigation, and speed of loading pages. Increasingly, there is more interest in conversion rates than CTRs. This is because the latter does not necessarily mean that there will be a high conversion number, and the two rates could even be an inverse relationship. When an ad motivates someone to click out of curiosity, it could lead to fewer sales, percentage-wise, than one geared toward getting qualified clicks

Learning the Work and Personal Skills Needed for Affiliate Marketing

Affiliate marketing relies on the same advertising methods as any other online business, such as search engine optimization (SEO), pay-per-click (PPC), display advertising, and e-mail marketing. Later chapters will more thoroughly cover these marketing tools. Each of these vehicles brings separate results and may have specific fees attached. SEO integrates keywords into your Web site. If customers are searching for the item your business is offering, this will increase the chance that they will find it easier and more quickly. PPC is an advertising method that allows you to set up your ad with keywords. Display ads integrate text, logos, photos, and video/audio media; this is done through either still or animated Web banners. E-mail ads are newsletters or updates sent to customers through electronic mail.

One successful method that affiliates use to boost traffic and sales is to concentrate on a small niche, that is, to pick a topic in conjunction with a product or service of considerable interest and build a Web site based on that theme. Next, they choose affiliates that align with the subject of their site and add these to the links in the text. By writing about the items from expert knowledge, the affiliate becomes a well-known, reliable source of material. The more a Web site attracts people who are interested in the topic, the greater the possibility they are going to purchase a product or service. In addition, the affiliates enjoy running their Web site, which will encourage them to put in more time. Overall, the whole process is quite simple: The site revolves around a topic that is of interest to both the affiliates and their visitors.

Beginners often believe that they just have to set up their Web site, submit their affiliate URL to the search engines, and they will be mobbed by visitors. They soon learn differently, as this is not the way that affiliates get large numbers of targeted visitors. Providing timely information that is of interest, that encourages users to come to the site and continually come back to read and learn more, has been proved time and time again to be an effective method. With a Web site that has up-to-date and valuable copy, affiliates are more likely to receive a good listing on the search engines, have a steady stream of targeted prospects, and promote their products and services. The relevancy of your Web site content to the product line is of utmost importance; you are not going to sell many motorcycle helmets to consumers who are looking for children's toys.

By providing visitors with information of value, affiliates establish themselves as people who have the expertise in their subject area, while also building an ongoing connection. Always remember the power of establishing a relationship. You have a much better opportunity to sell to someone who has become familiar with your site and with whom you have established trust. It is therefore essential that affiliates regularly question how they are presenting themselves. Are they including articles that appear professional, knowledgeable, and helpful? Do they give examples on the ways that these products and services provide value? Do they use these products? How? There is no magic bullet online for getting easy money. Affiliate programs do provide a great deal of income to many associates — if they accept the responsibility to put in the effort.

In short, if you want to be a successful Amazon Associate, you need to:

- Choose a topic of interest to you and to others.

- Determine your target audience.

- Decide on a select number of products of interest to market to this target audience.

- Develop an informative and interesting Web site that provides valuable copy, keeps your visitors coming back for more, and persuades them to click on your affiliate links and reach your location in a buying-ready mindset. If you already have a Web site, you have probably developed a topic of interest, whether it is parenting, jewelry, gardening, finance, real estate, sports, or technology. At Amazon, there are always corresponding books and products for whatever topic you choose. Thus, there certainly is a place for nearly every blog and Web site to make money selling topic-specific items.

Here are some mistakes that beginner affiliates often make:

- **Lack of persistence:** Many people believe that they are going to make thousands of dollars a week with just a little bit of work. Affiliate marketing can be lucrative, but it is a long-term effort that takes patience. Waiting for your first sale can seem like an eternity. Patience is a major aspect of affiliate marketing success. If you are going to be successful, you need to be willing and able to be patient. It may take one day to make your first sale, or it may take you a month or two; you cannot be the type of person who gives up easily. Take note that once you do make that first sale, the other ones will come much more easily.

- **Lack of consistency:** Similarly, it is necessary to devote a certain amount of time each day to the effort and to stick with one project until it is completed. Starting projects and never completing them will not work well. Stay with one item until it is finished and then go onto the next.

- **Lack of knowledge or interest:** You do not have to be an Internet guru, but you should understand the way that the online world works. You also need to have an interest in what you are promoting. Do not have a Web site about electronics only because you know they sell well; your visitors will see through you in a minute. They recognize passion, and they also know disinterest when it is presented.

With affiliate marketing, people all over the world leave their regular jobs and work at home as they please, just like many on-line ads promote. Yet, when the ads show the mansions, expensive cars, and beautiful beach vacation shots, there is something important that they do not tell you: All these people who have turned affiliate marketing into their "golden egg" have worked hard to do so. If you are looking for immediate, no-effort millions, affiliate marketing is not the answer. Yet, if you are ready to learn something new and exciting, and also invest consistent time and energy in return for good, steady income, affiliate marketing can meet your needs.

 # CHAPTER 12

Amazon's Renowned Associates Program

Amazon ranks as one of the best affiliate programs available. Because Amazon has established itself as a major online leader, Associates have a myriad of ways to bring in income. Amazon's Associate program stands out from other affiliate plans by offering millions of products from which to choose, industry leading conversion rates, and competitive referral fees that produce more money for Associates.

Amazon's Associate program is exceptionally attractive for other reasons as well. For example, you are able to create advertisements for products that are specific to your Web site.

If you run a Web site about video cameras, you can create advertisements with links to purchase the video cameras that you recommend. You can also create generic links; when someone purchases a product through the link that you generated, you will get a percentage of the sale. Most important, Amazon's Associate program is one of the oldest and most trusted affiliate programs across the globe. Millions of people are already familiar with the company and its products.

Over the years, the Amazon brand name has become a known entity throughout the world. There is no need to build reliability or credibility, and you need not convince the visitor of the value of the Amazon Web site. Associates earn referral fees when visitors follow links from their Web sites to Amazon to buy. These links can be for specific products, pages of search results, the Amazon homepage, or any other page at Amazon. Associates can also place product search boxes on their sites. Calculations for the referral fees are not done on the list price, but rather the sale price of every item that qualifies.

A product is only eligible to make a referral fee if the customer clicks the specified link from your Web site to Amazon and puts the item in his or her shopping cart, or buys it through Amazon's 1-Click feature. The session is over when one of the following occurs: (a) 24 hours goes by after the customer has clicked through, (b) the customer places an order for the item, or (c) the customer moves to a third-party's designated link. Amazon pays referral fees only on qualified products after the completion of the order, payment, and shipping.

Thus, referral fees are given on products that qualify that are put in a customer's shopping cart within 24 hours of going to Amazon by clicking on your link. This 24-hour window is no longer open when the customer orders an item or comes back to Amazon from another Web site. When the window closes, it is not possible to make referral fees on later purchases. Yet, if the customer then comes back to Amazon by using one of your links, another 24-

hour window is open. It is often the case that someone goes to Amazon from your Associates link, puts something in the shopping cart, and then leaves the site without ordering. If the item is in the customer's shopping cart some time within the 24-hour window, a referral fee will be given. You will not see the referral fee recorded on your account until the person actually buys the product, accepts the delivery, and pays Amazon in full.

The Classic Fee Structure and the Performance Fee Structure

Option One: Performance Fee Structure.

You earn the percentage as shown in the following table that corresponds to how many units sell. The referral rate will vary from 4 to 10 percent, which is based on your total number of items. This same rate applies to both Amazon and third-party merchandise, and to all referred items shipped throughout the month. See the following referral rate tier chart.

Referral-Fee Rates				
Total Items Shipped	CE Products	Kindle, Video on Demand, AmazonMP3, Game Downloads	Endless.com	General Products
1-6	4.00%	10.00%	15.00%	4.00%
7-30	4.00%	10.00%	15.00%	6.00%
31-110	4.00%	10.00%	15.00%	6.50%
111-320	4.00%	10.00%	15.00%	7.00%
321-630	4.00%	10.00%	15.00%	7.50%
631-1570	4.00%	10.00%	15.00%	8.00%
1571-3130	4.00%	10.00%	15.00%	8.25%
3131+	4.00%	10.00%	15.00%	8.50%

amazon.com

Amazon, Amazon.com and the Amazon.com logo are registered trademarks of Amazon.com, Inc. or its affiliates.

1. A **"CE Product"** is a qualifying product that is offered for sale in the "Electronics," "Audio and Video," or "Camera and Photo" sections of Amazon.

2. An **"Unbox Product"** is a qualifying product that is provided for sale in the "Unbox Video Downloads" section.

3. An **"Amazon MP3 Product"** is a qualifying product that is available for sale in the "MP3 Downloads" section.

4. A **"Kindle Product"** is a qualifying product that is a Kindle electronic reader device, book, or periodical subscription sold in the format for reading on a Kindle electronic reader device.

5. A **"Cell Phone with Service Product"** is a qualifying product consisting of a cell phone or other electronics device that can be used as a cell phone or wireless communication device, sold together with a wireless service plan that connects such a phone to a carrier's network.

6. A **"General Product"** is any qualifying product other than a CE, Kindle, Unbox, or Amazon MP3 Product, nor a gift certificate, and includes Cell Phone with Service Products. Amazon determines the classification of any qualifying products.

Option Two: Classic Fee Structure.

This is Amazon's fixed-referral-rate plan. You earn a 4 percent referral fee. Caps are placed on desktop and laptop computers. Referral fees are capped at $25, and Unbox video downloads are capped at $1.50 per item.

For both of these structures, the qualifying products and categories are:

- Apparel and Accessories
- Automotive
- Baby
- Beauty
- Books
- Camera and Photo
- Cell Phones and Service (phones only, not plans)
- Computers
- DVDs
- Electronics
- Gourmet Food
- Health and Personal Care
- Home and Garden
- Jewelry and Watches
- Kitchen and House Wares
- Magazine and Newspaper Subscriptions
- Music
- Musical Instruments
- Tools & Hardware
- Toys & Games Software
- Unbox Video Downloads
- Video

- Additional special items, such as the Kindle

The total number of qualifying product units, except for gift certificates, shipped in a calendar month will determine your "tier" level. This does not matter whether products are CE, Unbox, or general products. Once you reach a higher referral fee during the calendar month, this rate will apply as well as to units sold before you reach the next tier.

There are some exceptions to this. These are:

1. For gift certificate sales, you will receive 6 percent of revenues instead of the referral fee rates stated in the table.

2. There is a maximum referral fee of $25 per unit for personal computers.

3. You can only make a referral fee of $1.50 per item for all Unbox products, regardless of the revenues gained from the sale.

4. The referral fees for the AmazonMP3 products are a maximum of $1.50 per unit, even if revenues are higher.

5. Associates receive a $15 bonus added to the percentage of revenues for each Cell Phone with Service Product sold.

An Associate may select either the Classic Fee or Performance Fee Structure throughout the month. The selection deadline is

11:59 p.m. Pacific Time on the last day of each month. At the end of the month, the selection you had made most recently will be the one that is used for calculating your fees for the entire month. You will keep that enrollment plan for the next month unless canceling.

Amazon believes that the Performance Fee Structure is its most profitable choice, as it gives you the opportunity to receive higher fees when generating enough referrals. The more referrals you have, the better your earnings will be. Therefore, when you become a participant of the Associates program, you immediately are enrolled in the Performance Fee Structure. Amazon states that the extra earnings potential that the Performance Fee Structure provides will encourage Associates to begin sending a great deal of buyers to Amazon right after sending in their application.

> Amazon says that its compensation philosophy is simple: "Reward Associates for their contributions to our business in unit volume and in growth. Amazon is a fast growing business and we want our Associates to grow with us." — *From the Amazon Web site.*

You will receive your referral fees monthly. About 60 days after each calendar month ends, you will receive a check that covers the referral fees; a gift certificate for buying Amazon products; or a direct deposit into your bank account.

Time to Sign Up

To join the Associates program, you simply need to go to the Amazon Web site, scroll down to the bottom of the page, and click on the Amazon Associates link. You then fill out an electronic application with information on yourself and your Web site. Within a day or two, Amazon will respond and tell you whether or not you are accepted as an Associate. You should carefully read the "Operating Agreement." This stipulates that your product cannot do any of the following:

- Endorse sexually explicit materials.

- Condone violence.

- Sanction any discriminatory beliefs based on race, sex, religion, nationality, disability, sexual orientation, or age.

- Encourage illegal activities.

- Include "Amazon," any other trademark of Amazon. com, Inc. or its affiliates, or variations or misspellings of any of them, in their URLs to the left of the top-level domain name (e.g., ".com," ".net," and ".uk," just to name a few) — for example, a URL such as "amazon. mydomain.com," "amaozn.com," or "amazonauctions. net" would be unsuitable.

- Violate intellectual property rights in any other fashion.

Easy, Step-by-Step Registration Process

1. Click the "Join Now" button and you will be asked to sign in.

Amazon.com Associates Application

Becoming an Amazon Associate is a simple process. Amazon just requires you to enter the e-mail address that you are going to use for your account. This is the address that will be listed for your Associates account. It is where all you e-mail will be sent. If you are already using this address for an Amazon account, the same password can be used for your Associates account. If you would rather not have these accounts together, put down a different e-mail address.

2. You will then be asked to put in the contact information for where the payments should be sent.

Your Contact Information

Please enter contact information for the person or company to whom we should issue payments.

Note: Residents of North Carolina, or Rhode Island are not eligible to participate in the Associates program.

* Payee Name

Enter the name exactly as it should appear on the check. If the check is to be mailed to an individual other than the Payee, enter the name of the recipient in "Address 1" below

* Address Line 1

Address Line 2

Address Line 3

* City

* State, Province or Region

* ZIP or Postal Code

* Country [USA]

* Phone Number

* Contact same as Payee? ⦿ Yes
○ No

Your Web Site Profile: ⓘ

* What is the name of your Web site?

* What is the URL of the main Web site you use to send traffic to Amazon? [http://]

Which of the following topics best describes your main Web site(s)? [Please select]

* Briefly describe your site, including the type of items you intend to list.

Try to keep this under 10 lines or so.

Primary method for generating referrals [Content/Niche]

* Contract Terms ☐ You agree to the terms and condition of the Associates Operating Agreement

[Finish]

amazon.com

Amazon, Amazon.com and the Amazon.com logo are registered trademarks of Amazon.com, Inc. or its affiliates.

As you can see, it is easy to become an Amazon Associate. To process your application, you just need to provide the contact information for the person who will be receiving payments and for your Associate program account and information about the Web site that will become the affiliate location. You must enter your contact information, especially the name of the person or company that will receive the commissions generated from the Associate program and the address. You will also have to determine the category that will best describe your main Web site(s). These are:

- Apparel/Jewelry/Shoes
- Automotive/Transportation
- Business/Industrial
- Computers/Software/Technology/Photography
- Education/Reference/News
- Finance/Politics/Government
- Gaming/Grocery/Gourmet
- Home/Pets/Cooking/Weddings/Family/ Arts & Crafts
- Local Information
- Medical/Health/Beauty
- Movies/DVDs/TV
- Music/Music Downloads/MP3 Real Estate
- Religion/Ethnic
- Retail/General Merchandise
- Sports/Fitness/Outdoors Travel/Recreation
- Other

You must also list the types of products that you will be selling on your Web site(s) under these categories, and the primary method for generating referrals, such as by blog, comparison shopping engine, content/niche, or coupons/deals.

For tax purposes, you will need to fill out essential information. Because you are earning income through the Associate program, you must report any earnings over $400. Amazon will need your tax ID name, tax ID number, and organization type. If you are a single proprietor or individual earning extra income, the tax ID number is your social security number, and the organization type is individual. If you have never had your own business in the past, you should talk with a local accountant or tax attorney about small business accounting.

Depending on your state, for example, you may need a license and have to pay state taxes on earnings. Quarterly payments to the federal government are required after a specified amount of earnings, and a fine is accrued if this is not followed. It is also advised that you keep your business and personal accounts and corresponding credit cards and expenses completely separate. If you want to expand your business at any time in the future, your personal credit will not be accepted by a bank. You need to establish business credit.

When signing up for Amazon, you will also have to identify how you want your payments to be sent. This can be through paper checks, direct-deposit into your bank account, or through an Amazon gift certificate. There are several advantages to choosing to be paid by direct deposit instead of by check:

- The minimum payment is just $10 for direct deposit, compared to $100 for checks.

- Amazon deducts a $15 processing fee from all monthly checks sent to the Associates, but it is free for payment through direct deposit or gift certificates.

- Payments made as direct deposits are safe and deposited into your bank account three to seven days faster than paper checks.

If your billing address is outside the United States and the direct deposit is unavailable to you, Amazon will waive the $15 fee.

Your Payee Tax Information

* Tax Name

Required for U.S. citizens, residents and corporations.

* Tax ID Number

Payee Tax Information (for U.S. citizens or residents)
Please enter your U.S. Social Security number (for individuals) or Federal U.S. tax ID (for corporations). Learn More

* Organization Type None ▼

Your Payment Method

○ **Pay me by Amazon.com gift certificate/card**
($10 minimum earnings)

○ **Pay me by direct deposit**
($10 minimum earnings)
(Is this safe for international associates? Learn more)

Note: if you have successfully saved your direct deposit information, then secure fields such as bank account number and routing code will appear blank to protect your personal information. If you want to update your direct deposit payment information, you will have to reenter the data for these fields.
Bank Location

US **USA**

Bank Name
	true

Bank Account Holder Name
	true

Bank Account Type
Please select ▼

Bank Account Number (What's this?)
	true	2	17

Routing Number / ABA Number (What's this?)
	true	9	9

○ **Pay me by check**
($100 minimum earnings. Note a $15 processing fee will be applied to all Associates with U.S. addresses when choosing this option.)

amazon.com

Amazon, Amazon.com and the Amazon.com logo are registered trademarks of Amazon.com, Inc. or its affiliates.

More than One Account

You are allowed to use a single account password and Associates ID for numerous Web sites. Just list each of your Web sites in the description field in "Your Associates Account Information." If it is necessary to have separate reporting for each site, go to "Your Account" and click on the "Manage your Tracking ID" link, and ask for separate tracking IDs for each site. Amazon allows you as many as 100 tracking IDs per Associate account. If you have further requirements, you will need to contact the Associate program customer service department. It is not recommended that you create an Associate account for each Web site. It will be much easier for you to keep track of your earnings if you use a single account.

CHAPTER 13

The Grand Opening of an Amazon aStore

Would you love to have an online store that highlights Amazon products? What about having this store ready to go live within minutes? aStore by Amazon offers this store along with a quick setup. Within a day, you can be selling the same featured items as businesses with many years of merchandising experience.

There are two major aspects of running any business. The first is the marketing and merchandising to your customers. If you have no one to buy your products or services, having a store is a moot point. Build it, and they may not come; if it does not cater to people's needs, they will come but may not return. There are hundreds of thousands of stores where visitors come only one time and then go off and try something else. Amazon is giving you the opportunity to open a truly successful store within a short period of time. You can rely on its decade of experience and millions of customers who are already buying their products.

Second, you need products. With aStore, you do not have to find and pay a vendor to supply the merchandise, have these items shipped, and worry about storage. All you have to do is hang up your shingle or put your domain on the server, and you are open for business. Of course, you have to market, and the competition is keen. That is true for any online business. Nonetheless, even here, Amazon helps you out. It offers suggestions on how best to market your new enterprise and also does some of the marketing for you by continuing to spread its positive reputation.

amazon.com

Amazon, Amazon.com and the Amazon.com logo are registered trademarks of Amazon.com, Inc. or its affiliates.

What is the aStore?

The aStore is an Associate product that gives you the power to create a professional online store in minutes, which can be embedded within or linked to your Web site without the need for programming skills. If you enjoy making referrals in your area of interest and find that a number of your readers are purchasing products based on your recommendations, why lose the benefits of these sales? You can create an aStore, which is an e-commerce business in which you put Amazon's merchandise up for sale, and you design the store with your own selection of items from the numerous company products. After setting the site up, you will keep visitors longer and make referral commissions. Any member of the Associates program can use the aStore tool.

Whether you are selling on Amazon yet or not, you can still make money with an Amazon aStore. All you have to do is sign up with Amazon's Associates program, and you can quickly have an e-commerce enterprise virtually on anything on the Web, using a variety of widgets and links. With the aStore, there is a collection of products you choose, categorize, and display on your own Web site or blog. You can customize the look of the store quite easily, and if you are familiar with editing .css files, it is easy to get creative with the fonts and layout. The aStore allows Amazon Associates to configure an entire online store in a few easy steps. It gives customers the shopping experience they expect and can contain selected product groups — or an entire product range offered by Amazon. This store can be integrated into an Associate's Web site with a single line of HTML code. The store also offers many of the features available on the Amazon Web site, such as search, customer reviews, and similar products.

How Does the aStore Work?

Integrating aStore is simple. To create and configure the store, the Associate only needs to complete a few forms. Then, the Associate receives a single line of code that he or she can copy and paste into the appropriate section of their Web site. The "Get Link" step of the configuration process will provide a single line of HTML code that needs to be copied to the Associate's Web site. The HTML code can be integrated into an iframe on the Web site or placed directly in a page with sufficient space to show the complete store. There are no programming skills needed to create or integrate aStore into a Web site; the key feature of this tool is its complete ease of use. The development process is self-explanatory and can be completed in a short amount of time. Depending on the level of customization required to match the store to layout of an Associate's Web site, setting it up may take from only a couple of minutes to a quarter of an hour.

Amazon offers several choices and ways to integrate and publish an aStore: Link directly to your aStore as a stand-alone site; embed your aStore using an inline frame; and integrate your aStore using a frameset for Web sites using frame layout structure. If you own a normal HTML-based Web site, integration of the aStore into the Web site is straightforward and simple: Just create a link directly to the aStore or a new page, insert the Amazon iframe or frame layout embedding code to the new page, and link to this page from your main index page. If you are blogging on the WordPress® platform, integrating Amazon aStore with WordPress can be somewhat more difficult. Yet aStore and WordPress can still be integrated by using WordPress' page template. The aStore will appear inside the framework or layout of WordPress without having to use a WordPress plug-in.

Amazon also lets you customize your aStore to match the layout of your Web site. You have the choice of a wide range of colors for matching borders, fields, lines, text, and background to the color scheme of your own online site. There is no good or bad aStore concept; it just comes down to the individual entrepreneur and his or her merchandising skills, business skills, and commitment level. Smaller Web sites that are tailored to the interests of their users can be as successful as larger Web sites with a great deal of traffic; niche Web sites can be as lucrative as those that offer a wide range of assortment of merchandise.

In fact, Associates should try to make the aStore match the layout of their own Web sites. A well-integrated Web site will lead to better results, as visitors will feel more comfortable with the experience. aStore also allows you to offer your customers a shopping cart for multiple item purchases, as Amazon is already one of the most trusted stores online for checking out. If you have a blog about pet supplies, for example, you can sell Amazon products that correlate with this blog. The object is to find a good niche with a high profit potential and build the aStore to take advantage of it.

The aStore is a shopping venture you can integrate into your own online presence, selling products from Amazon that you think your visitors may find of interest. For example, if you have a Web site about music, you could set up different categories, such as rock, hip hop, heavy metal, or mellow, and let Amazon automatically display a list of top-selling CDs from its range, with prices, cover images, information, and reviews. The use of the widgets, such as the MP3 and video, add to the entire look and interest for the potential buyers. Visitors to your store can stay around a while by reading the blog, making comments, seeing the products uniquely displayed, adding items to their shopping cart, and then, when ready, be taken to the Amazon Web site for secure and safe purchasing. You will receive reports regularly, so you can see specifically what any changes are bringing to your Web site in terms of visitors and purchases made on your site or elsewhere.

The aStore also features Amazon and third-party products listed on Amazon only. Some aStore owners, for example, have followed the early lead of Amazon and sold books. Some of these store owners have written their own books, and others only sell publications by other authors who they believe their visitors would like. Amazon Associates can easily set up international stores on their site as well. They simply need to sign up separately for the different Associates Programs, build their stores for each locale, and integrate the stores into their Web site. Appropriate links in the Web site's navigation can then link to the stores of different geographies.

Here is how aStore makes this an enticing option:

- It is easy to build.

- Amazon hosts it on its servers, but you can use it on your own site.

- The steps to create a store are clear.

- There are numerous options. You can create a link to your stand-alone store on Amazon, embed the store in your own site with iframes, or use HTML frames to include with your own Web site.

- When visitors click a product in your store, it loads all of Amazon's information within the same page.

- Amazon's widgets give you the opportunity to use — or not use — features such as your Amazon Wish List, Listmania readers' lists, similar items, accessories, customer reviews, and editorial reviews. Everything except for the reviews appear on your Web site sidebars,

— which may or may not be part of the body copy, depending what you would like for your design.

It is a good idea to test a product before investing a lot of time and money into it. One way that you can do that is to use Amazon's aStore. You can list for free whatever products you want from Amazon's vast catalog of products. The good part is that there is no cost, and it is easy to start. The bad part is that you will not make nearly as much money per item shipped as you would with drop-shipping and your own store, and it is also a tough task to get an aStore to look custom-designed. Still, it can be an excellent choice for a brand-new Web site that is still building traffic, and it can give you an idea of interest for your product line.

As with any other business, there is no guarantee that you will quickly make a lot of money from running an Amazon aStore. But it does have a lot of possibilities, all based on how you use it. Ultimately, the success of the aStore for your Web site will be based on several parameters, including your ability to get your visitors to feel confident about buying from your store, and how well you integrate the aStore and product links into your other online sites. As noted on the Associates Program agreement, partners using aStore are paid according to the usual Associates referral.

Here is the easy step-by-step process for setting up your store:

- Look for and find the specific products you would like to show on your Web site. Add the required category pages.

- Name the page.

- Choose a customized concept or make changes to color and design the section of the page with Amazon.

- Decide on a sidebar that runs on the left or right.

- Choose the widgets/options to show for the sidebar of each page.

- Click "finish and get link." You will have a simple link for your Web site or a link that will embed your site in an inline frame or frameset link

CASE STUDY: ASHA & VISHAL WADHER

Asha Wadher, President
Vishal Wadher, CTO
Atmosphere Solutions
600 East Baseline Road, Suite B-9
(602) 324-3489
www.atmospheresolutions.com

As an Amazon Associate, you can create your own Web site using Amazon's tutorial. There are also a number of Associates who want to take that extra step and make their site a little different from the norm, have more capabilities, or get marketing support. Atmosphere Solutions has teamed up with Amazon as an e-commerce WebStore service developer to create creative Amazon online store solutions with unique features.

Asha Wadher, having worked in the hospitality industry, has gained a strong background in business management and customer relations. Her brother, Vishal, brings the other half of the equation in Information technology: Internet marketing, Network Administration, Custom Software Development and Project

Management. "In 2006, we heard that Amazon was looking for high-quality vendors as partners for the WebStore Division," recalls Vishal Wadher. "We saw this as a great opportunity, as it further complemented services provided by Atmosphere Solutions."

Since then, the Wadher siblings have helped a variety of Web Store owners with Web strategies, e-mar-keting and custom software development.

CASE STUDY: ASHA & VISHAL WADHER

For example, Euro Mattresses, of Somycol in Miami, turned to Atmosphere Solutions to design a WebStore, as well as get help with the technical backend of the online business. Wildflax in Las Vegas, which sells natural food supplements, turned to Atmosphere Solutions to create a customized design for a look different from the norm.

The firm will work with new WebStore businesses that have a business plan and are ready to launch into e-commerce. Atmosphere Solutions also teams with long-tenure companies that have wanted to branch out into other online areas. There is a one-time charge to design the WebStore, according to the customer's specifications. Additional charges are accrued for online marketing solutions, such as search engine optimization, and design updates and changes.

Why go with an Amazon partner rather than work solely with the template provided to build a WebStore? "With an Amazon WebStore template, Associates can build the basic foundation of their store. However, it will look similar to most other WebStores. Also, although the template is easy to use, many companies just do not have the time or skills to create a customized and professional design to reflect their brand identity. They want to focus on their business and leave the IT work to us. We can also give Associates a great customized look by adding Flash animation, custom images, music, or video that they want," explains Vishal Wadher.

CHAPTER 14

Using Theme, Color, and Widgets

Once you register as an Amazon Associate, you can immediately begin to use Amazon's link builder tool to create links to specific products on your Web site. Generating revenue with the Amazon Associates program is all about choosing the right type of ads and links for the right product(s) and placing them in the right place and context. You can also use Amazon's contextual products, which will place links to products on your site based on what words are on the page. This is a good way to automatically target your readers' interests. There is also a whole new set of widget links that are available to keep customers on your Web site longer. Amazon is continually changing and adding on to these widgets to keep the customers interested and increase purchases. As a member of the Associates Program, you will have access to Associates Central®, where you will create links, see traffic and earning reports, and find news regarding the latest offerings from Amazon. According to Amazon, the Associates Central allows you to:

- Use the "build links" tool to design and place links to Amazon.

- Keep track of traffic and earnings reports on a daily basis.

- Pay no revenue share.

- Have no ongoing licensing requisites.

- Modify your Web site any time, live.

- Host on your Web site or the hosting account.

- Take advantage of the easy-to-use shopping cart, where buyers add desired products to their cart and only leave your Web site when they are finished shopping and ready for Amazon checkout.

- Market merchandise and categories in the page titles.

- Update Web site templates easily.

- Manage your site pages easily with the HTML editor for customized store content.

The most lucrative approach is for you to feature products that best match your Web site's theme and the interests of your visitors. For example, if your site is about wine, you might want to promote the latest book about wineries in Italy. Remember the following tips when choosing your products:

- **Select products that match your Web site content.** Limit your choices by looking on Amazon for specific products, keywords, and categories that match the subject of your Web site. View your results first by product line, then sort by other criteria, such as sales rank or average customer review.

- **Think about product cross-merchandising.** A large number of your visitors will have an interest in a wide variety of products. You can take advantage of this diversity by marketing items from throughout the varied Amazon catalog and, thus, capture more sales. For instance, if you have been highlighting best-selling exercise equipment on your Web site, consider increasing your sales by featuring additional pertinent products, such as nutritional supplements or workout apparel.

- **Search for other items to feature with Amazon's similarities service.** On the detail page of a product that you have already identified as appropriate for your Web site, click on the "Explore Similar Items" link to find additional items. For example, customers who buy kitchen items may also want to buy products for outdoor cooking.

- **Review your orders report** to determine which products customers buy after visiting your Web site. In order to not lose these sales, you may want to market some of these items directly yourself. Spend time gaining additional information about the best ways to analyze and utilize the report's information.

- **Conduct a trial on selling higher-priced products.** Highlighting a range of priced items offers you the opportunity to increase your commissions.

Using the Amazon Visual Links

As noted, Amazon continuously updates its technology and is normally on the forefront of both what occurs on the Web site itself and also behind the scenes. In 2008, the company added a number of new widgets. Although small, they are visually effective and easy-to-use electronic links that give you the opportunity to highlight special items from Amazon on your site, blog, and social networking pages, such as Facebook® and MySpace®. In just a matter of a minute or two, you can add these widgets to you or your visitors' favorite Amazon products, along with your personal comments about these items. You can also choose from a range of colors and design themes that match the subject of your Web site.

These widgets can highlight music, movies, food, clothing, entertainment, and many other themes that may be of interest to the million visitors going to Web sites that carry Amazon Associates links. In 2007 alone, Amazon Associates created more than 200,000 unique widgets that were displayed more than 800 million times.

Amazon Widgets

The traditional and state-of-the-art Amazon widgets include:

Search

These widgets allow visitors to find and explore products of interest without leaving the Associate's Web site. Visitors can use the
"search box" if you have a lot of products displayed on a page.
When a top search engine, such as Google®, Yahoo!®, or Bing®
sends someone to a Web site, and that person does not automatically see the expected product, there is a tendency to quickly go
on to the next possible site. In the meantime, your sale is lost. If
there is a centrally located search box, the visitor is most apt to
use it and not leave.

Quick Linker

Users can quickly and easily link to relevant products while writing their blog posts or page content with the use of these custom
HTML tags.

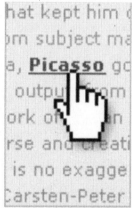

amazon.com

*Amazon, Amazon.com and the Amazon.com logo are registered
trademarks of Amazon.com, Inc. or its affiliates.*

Omakase

Omakase ads and links are one of the latest widgets. They feature products based on page content. According to Amazon, the Japanese word omakase means "leave it up to us." It is frequently said in Japanese restaurants when the chef uses expertise and cooking knowledge to choose and make the food for a customer without being given any directions. Omakase links are designed to show potential customers products they would most likely buy, which depends on Amazon's awareness of the Web site and its visitors, and the actual page.

To design omakase links, you will need to change the template and appearance elements, as well as copy the resulting code on your page. Associates now have options for modifying the layout and adapting the ads to match the look and feel of their Web site, coordinating with the site and supporting their brand by selecting the background colors, links, and border colors and also the use of text or images.

You will be able to get into the omakase links area the same way as with any other widgets. Log onto your account and click on "Build Links." You will see a range of different applications you can use to customize the Web site. Take note that the omakase links have to perform a technical search of your Web site for pertinent copy. Amazon scans the pages and then picks and adds the most appropriate products.

If you have installed technical safety systems on your Web site, this technical search may not be able to be performed. It may also keep link's features from proper operations. Amazon may then choose not to supply the content to your Web site because it is not possible to do the necessary search. You must make sure that the "privacy information" link is displayed and not obscured when putting on omakase links. Amazon has the right to cancel your Associates Program affiliation if you do not prominently use the privacy information link.

Omakase links uniquely combine information on each Associate's Web site according to the visitor's taste, the site's content, and historical trends to dynamically generate relevant ads that Amazon then serves to your site. With easy-to-use and strong customization options, omakase lets you automatically provide personalized product ads to your Web site visitors that complement online design. Because omakase optimizes on more than just the page itself, Associates may see a range of different products in their links, but they will also find that the links are based on what their visitors would like to buy. Actually, because the goal of omakase is to show the right product to the right person, everyone visiting the site may see different products.

Omakase Links

Their slogan is "Leave it up to us!" These automatically feature ideal products based on Amazon's unique knowledge about what works for your site, for your users and for the content of your page.

amazon.com

Amazon, Amazon.com and the Amazon.com logo are registered trademarks of Amazon.com, Inc. or its affiliates.

To determine what products to show on your page, omakase uses a number of different techniques. One of these methods involves the omakase system that processes text on your page and finds products from Amazon that relate to the theme. Amazon also uses unique information about the products that have proved success-ful for the Associate in the past; and, if the person viewing the site is an Amazon customer, the ads can be tailored to that user's interests. Here are some of the specific options you have:

- Control the branding for the ad, with a choice between showing Amazon as a logo or as text.

- Modify text, borders, and background color and run banners with or without small product images, text, and borders.

- Use the banner size option to determine the dimen-sions of the ad based on pixel count.

- Automatically see the display size and products in a preview when changes are made.

- Choose whether to display both the Amazon and lowest Marketplace price by third parties or just the one from Amazon, and also if the display will show the amount that the product is being discounted (for those items larger than 10 percent).

- Modify colors of text to highlight the author, artist, or brand name of the product.

- Automatically identify and link relevant phrases within your blog page content to Amazon products, providing new ad inventory and saving you the time from needing to manually create links. You can add the customized links to your pages in minutes. This is a helpful tool if you have a lot of content and not have much time to thoroughly pick and add the most appropriate products.

- Embed the affiliate links as part of your content.

- Choose the best products and display them. The omakase tool can crawl your page, identify the critical keywords, and start displaying appropriate content. At this point, you have a choice between using omakase and/or context links.

Product Previews

Product previews provide a gateway right from your Web site to Amazon. When visitors put their mouse over a text or image preview-enhanced link, a small window pops up with pertinent copy and information regarding the item you are displaying, such as product image, new and used prices, average customer review, and availability. Product previews give visitors the opportunity to see valuable merchandise information without having to travel onto Amazon. At this point, from the product window, users have the option to put the product in their shopping cart or click through to get more information on Amazon's Web site. Product previews allow you to give your visitors an easy and effortless way to put products in their shopping cart while reading your site's content. Results from tests find that there are high click-through and conversion rates from those who see a product preview. This is certainly a good choice in conjunction with context links and text links.

amazon.com

Recommended Products

Recommended product widgets are dynamic links where Amazon automatically selects and serves the content. You enter the type of products you want displayed, and Amazon will update them with the best-selling items, based on your stated criteria. Because Amazon automatically updates these links with the latest content, there is less work required on your part to keep your links and banners updated. For ease and flexibility, you can build recommended product links in two different ways — by category and by keyword — each in multiple sizes.

Amazon, Amazon.com and the Amazon.com logo are registered trademarks of Amazon.com, Inc. or its affiliates.

Further, by changing their background, text, and link color, you can customize these links to best fit the design and layout of your site. Based on a product category or keyword, a random set of products are displayed to the visitors. This is appropriate if your Web site content is quite generic but related to a high-level category such as electronics or apparel. Note that there are more targeted options available for other purposes.

Context Links

Context links are similar to the omakase, except they are relevant phrases instead of being content-based. These are directly merged into your content. It is best to use these widgets when there is a lot of user-generated content on your Web site, such as forums, or if you do not have a lot of time to pick specific products and link them on your Web site. Also, one of the positive things about context links, omakase, and recommended product widgets is that even after a couple of months or years, they will continue to display the most up-to-date and available products; you do not have to be concerned about removing any of the specific products that are no longer available.

Context links automatically look for and link contextually relevant phrases within your content to Amazon products. These widgets can be designed as conventional links or in such a way that when a user hovers over them, a small window appears and shows a preview of the appropriate product from Amazon. It is believed that this widget unlocks new ad inventory for Associates by identifying linking opportunities that were not previously noted. It also gives you the opportunity to control the location and number of links on each page. In addition, context links can save you the time required to manually create text links within your content. With context links, merchants can also determine:

- The number of links desired on each page.

- Which part of the page is to be linked.

- What Amazon product categories are linked.

- Whether to match exact product names only.

- Whether to opt for choices of single underline, dashed underline, and double underline link formats to let your Web site visitors know they are context links.

amazon.com

Amazon, Amazon.com and the Amazon.com logo are registered trademarks of Amazon.com, Inc. or its affiliates.

Text Links

Text links give you full control. You can pick a product or keyword of your choice and create a highly targeted page on Amazon. Use this option if you normally review or write about a particular topic and you have identified an excellent product that goes along with it. If the review is specifically about an item itself, then this widget would be ideal. If your content can include an image as well, then go with the product links. Some blog software like WordPress does not allow placing JavaScript™ or iframe tags, and this restricts the links to text links.

Amazon, Amazon.com and the Amazon.com logo are registered trademarks of Amazon.com, Inc. or its affiliates.

Product Links

Product links are similar to text links. In situations in which you want to target visitors, you have the option of picking the exact product or having the possibility of multiple products with one shown at random. These are appropriate for content that centers on a specific product or topic so that the related product(s) goes along with it.

Carousel

Carousel widgets take your products for a circular spin. With this widget, visitors see products displayed in a 3D carousel or Ferris wheel display. You can suggest certain products to be shown or have the most up-to-date bestsellers and new releases from any Amazon category you want appear.

Briefly, the carousel gives you a unique way to advertise several related Amazon products at the same time. The carousel can be set up vertically or horizontally and at three different dimensions. Also, the products can be chosen automatically by category, or loaded statically up front.

Amazon, Amazon.com and the Amazon.com logo are registered trademarks of Amazon.com, Inc. or its affiliates.

Deals

The deals widget displays the hottest golden deals from Amazon on your Web page, so you can decide which Gold Box deals you want to specifically feature. You can delight your viewers with the "Deal of the Day," "Lightning Deals," or "Our Best Deals" from across Amazon.

Deal of the Day: One product or a set of closely related products on sale for that date only.

Our Best Deals: Several different sale items and continuous promotions throughout Amazon.

Lightning Deals: One product matched with a restricted number of bonus savings coupons good for four hours, or the customers have used all coupons.

Quick Picks: Items designed each day particularly for your site, matched with coupons that have a have a limited-time offer for extra savings.

Amazon, Amazon.com and the Amazon.com logo are registered trademarks of Amazon.com, Inc. or its affiliates.

Slideshow

The slideshow widget lets you make a fashion slideshow from the images of products in the Amazon catalog. Pick your favorite books, movies, or CD covers — or show the latest bread maker and food blender. Slideshow widgets let you add your own comments to each image and customize the show to suit your Web page and pictures. Create a slideshow yourself in three quick steps:

1. Choose and sort your product images by entering your terms in the search box. You can search the entire Amazon catalog or only within a selected Amazon store. When you find the products that interest you, click "add product" to have them shown in your widget. You can add comments to your selected products (Make sure you hit the "Save Comments" button), and drag and drop the products to rearrange their order in the list.

2. Hit the "Next step" button and customize your widget's appearance. Tailor the colors and layout of your link to fit the page design and theme. You can choose the format of your slideshow — simple, gallery, or scrolling — and also the size of the widget. You can also decide which style of slide transition you think looks best.

3. Add the widget to your page. Then, when you are pleased with the final look, hit "Add to My Web page" to get it onto your site.

amazon.com

Amazon, Amazon.com and the Amazon.com logo are registered trademarks of Amazon.com, Inc. or its affiliates.

Product Cloud

This widget displays a cluster full of different product titles that relate to your Web site page. The size of the font in the cloud displays its degree of relevance to other products on your site. The larger titles are more closely aligned with your products in your store. When someone hovers a mouse over any title, it will show more information about that specific product. This widget is ideal for those Web sites that have changing content, such as blog pages. It will keep up with your transforming page by automatically showing new titles as your page evolves. To make a product cloud link, merely choose whether the widget should select items from the entire Amazon catalog or only display those from a single Amazon product category. Then, go ahead and design how you want the cloud link to look, and add it to your page. The first time you install this widget, it may take a few minutes before it displays relevant titles because the Amazon system is analyzing your page.

amazon.com

Listmania

Listmania links include any list that you make on Amazon. With a copy, paste, and click, you have a perfect widget for your blog. Here is how it is done: Go to Amazon and copy the address for any Listmania list, such as *The New York Times*® Book Review Best Sellers. Now, go to the widget gallery and choose Amazon from the list on the left. Select Listmania from the options that appear. Paste the Web address for the Listmania list into the box and click the "GO" button. Your widget will then appear. Click the "Grab This Widget" button to configure the widget and install it on your blog, Web site, or social page. In the configuration screen, you will be able to appropriately adjust the title and layout — you can customize it to perfectly fit your site. This list link has all of the advantages that make widgets so useful: It is easy to install, can be customized to fit your site, updates automatically, and generates revenue via Associate Web sites.

To create your Listmania widget, enter the link to an Amazon Listmana List:

Listmania

Don't worry! AdaptiveBlue will never keep or share your information. Read our privacy policy. GO

amazon.com

Amazon, Amazon.com and the Amazon.com logo are registered trademarks of Amazon.com, Inc. or its affiliates.

Shopping Cart

Shopping cart links add products directly to your customers' shopping carts. They make the buying process more convenient and usually convert considerably better than those to product detail pages. You can build add-to-cart links in several ways:

- **Enhanced product links:** These use Amazon links such as product image, title, price, and an add-to-cart button. All you have to do is copy the code to your site.

- **Add-to-cart buttons:** These create an add-to-cart button on your Web site for items offered by Amazon by copying and modifying a code. Select from several styles of graphical buttons. You can create similar add-to-cart forms for items offered by third-party sellers using Amazon Web Services.

- **Amazon e-commerce service remote shopping cart:** This option gives you maximum amount of control and influence over your visitors' shopping experience. Amazon Web Services can build a remote Amazon shopping cart on your Web site. As visitors browse your site, they will be able to add products to their cart without having to leave the page. When they are finally ready to complete their order, the contents of their cart will be available at Amazon for secure checkout.

Any Page

You may provide a link on your Web site that will link to any particular page on the Amazon site, as long as you have accurately used the special link formats.

MP3 Clips

MP3 clips widget, one of the newest links, lets visitors play samples of songs from Amazon's huge digital rights management (DRM)-free catalog of more than five million MP3s. You can choose specific songs and albums to display on your Web site, or show the most current bestsellers and latest releases from any music genre you decide on.

This MP3 widget plays 30-second music clips of songs or albums, which you can determine or select from the Amazon list of bestsellers by category. If you do not want to select the songs, Amazon looks at the most recent MP3 buying history of Associates on the widget configuration page. Anyone visiting your sites only has to click on the widget and go to a page to buy the song or album they want. This can be an excellent enhancement for many Associates' sites. For instance, the Associate can change songs that go along with the season or events. There are a lot of opportunities. The MP3 widget can be configured for sidebars (120×300 or 160×300 pixels) or a larger size for integration with content. After the MP3 widget is built, you will have the choice to get instructions for how to insert it into several social networks and blogs, or to grab the code to and paste into the site.

amazon.com

Amazon, Amazon.com and the Amazon.com logo are registered trademarks of Amazon.com, Inc. or its affiliates.

MP3 Widget Reviews:

"The Amazon affiliate program has a new MP3 widget that really sets them apart from other affiliate programs. Fan blogs of different singers and bands are a natural. Movie sites can feature soundtracks. There are a lot of possibilities here," said Shawn Collins, co-founder of the Affiliate Summit.

Martin Stiksel, **www.Last.fm** co-founder, said: "When we started offering millions of tracks for free-on-demand streaming earlier this year, we were confident that enabling music fans to listen for free would encourage more music purchasing. In this respect, our relationship with Amazon MP3 was vital – it has the breadth of catalogue and ease of use that's necessary to give our users the best online music consumption experience. We were extremely pleased to see that our partnership has raised the game for online music, as download and CD purchasing on Last.FM via Amazon increased 119 percent since the free-on-demand launch. This is a great vindication for the pioneering services both our companies provide to music fans."

Preview Player

The preview player allows you to display and/or publicly perform on your Web site certain video and static media content via data feeds that are made available by Amazon.

amazon.com

Amazon, Amazon.com and the Amazon.com logo are registered trademarks of Amazon.com, Inc. or its affiliates.

Video

With the video widget links, you can add product links to the videos you already posted on your Web page.

Unbox

Unbox video widgets show studio previews for a tremendous variety of current and classic movies or TV shows, which Unbox video download service offers. This is an area that continues to grow under Amazon's enterprise.

amazon.com

Amazon, Amazon.com and the Amazon.com logo are registered trademarks of Amazon.com, Inc. or its affiliates.

Many Amazon Associates display product links to easily show one item with its image, product name, and up-to-date prices.

Because you want numerous repeat visitors to your Web site and do not have much space allotted to these widgets, you have an interesting way to promote and inform at the same time. You can also provide variety by configuring your product links so they randomly display one of several items, rather than displaying only one. With the link customization options, you can specify options like colors. Then, change this HTML to feature other Amazon products that may also be of interest to your Web site visitors. After you paste the changed HTML into your Web site, then each time the page loads, one of the included items will be selected and shown randomly to visitors.

Listed products will be randomly selected for display each time the page loads. Now that there are so many different widgets that are tailored to the individual customers and that work on formats like carousels, videos and MP3s, variety is indeed the spice of life on Amazon Associates' Web sites.

A Widget by any Other Name

The term widget can be extremely confusing, especially when there are many other words that are used that mean the same thing. Many times, the word "link" is used in place of widget, although they are different. Widgets are also called "buttons" and "gadgets." According to the tech-savvy blog of Niall Kennedy, the term "widget" is a generic term for a manufactured object that comes from the 1924 Broadway play "Beggar on Horseback." It is an object that has no value, but is produced for common usage. The main character in the play is torn between his poor living as an artist creating things he enjoys or a job in a factory creating meaningless "widgets." In economics, the term "widget" is used as a generic object that should not distract from the example at hand. There is the reference to Bob's Widget Shop instead of Bob's Donut Shop to focus on the growth numbers, optimum pricing, and additional economic aspects where the details of a donut are irrelevant.

The word "widget" also describes the basic building blocks of a desktop operating system's graphical user interface. Desktop application developers can take advantage of standard user interface libraries such as a menu, buttons, or display pane. Ralph Swick and Mark Ackerman of Massachusetts Institute of Technology used the word widget for the X Window System in 1988. The term is still used today in the desktop development space to describe building new user interfaces. Amazon launched its own "Amazon Widgets" in 2007. There are now 21 widgets and counting.

(Source: Niall Kennedy, "Weblog," September 30, 2007)

CHAPTER 15

Reports with Amazon Associates

A mazon Associates' reports reflect each individual affiliate's earnings. These reports are posted daily for any affiliate referrals and earnings during the previous day of business. Because the reports are posted daily, they are not live. You cannot obtain any data for the current day until the following day, when Amazon posts its daily report.

Reports for a particular day are normally posted by 9 a.m. on the following day. These reports are often posted even earlier. However, there are times when they are available much later, especially on days when there is heavy traffic to Amazon. The reason why reports are posted at unpredictable times is that Amazon runs batch processes that are dependent on computer load and traffic volume, and sometimes, there are glitches in the code. To eliminate the need for frequent visits to Amazon Associates Central, Amazon developed an e-mail notification service that lets you know the moment Amazon Associates' report is posted.

Being able to analyze and act on Amazon's easy-to-read reports is critical to the success of the Associates. Amazon offers extensive data about the activity of your various links to encourage you to optimize your performance in the program, try different techniques, and find which one works best. This information consists of data on your traffic, revenue, earnings, conversion rates, and link types. Reports are updated every 24 hours, ensuring that you have up-to-date information. Below is an example of the report provided to Associates.

amazon.com

Amazon, Amazon.com and the Amazon.com logo are registered trademarks of Amazon.com, Inc. or its affiliates.

Obtaining Information on Customers

In addition to looking at the absolute number of orders, you can also compare product-link conversion for merchandise that you promote on your Web site. The reports display the number of clicks for each product that occurred through a product link or add-to-cart button, number of orders placed through the product links, and the resulting product link conversion. You can also see the items that were ordered after customers clicked through to other Amazon pages.

For certain link types, Amazon can count an impression whenever one of your Amazon links is viewed. You receive a report on the number of impressions your Amazon links receive by link type in the Link-Type Report. You can utilize this information to gain a better understanding of those links that are the most effective in generating traffic and determine which links you can better use to maximize your performance and earnings. The Orders Report combines click and order information. In the top "Items with Orders" section, you are able to view each item ordered and how many direct-link clicks it received. Below the ordered items, you can find an "Items with No Orders" section.

When you click the arrow next to "Show All Items," you can see a list of items that were viewed via a direct link but not ordered. In the summary at the bottom of the report, you may see a number of "Other Clicks." These are clicks from other link types, including links to the homepage, links to search results, recommended product links, and links to the main landing page for each product category. Use the Link-Type Report to see how each link type is performing for your Web site.

Earnings Report Totals   Glossary

January 1, 2006 to January 31, 2006

	Items Shipped	Revenue	Referral Fees
Total Amazon.com Items Shipped	4	$66.14	$3.94
Total Third Party Items Shipped	10	$231.34	$14.54
Total Items Shipped	**14**	**$297.48**	**$18.48**
Total Items Returned	**0**	**$0.00**	**$0.00**
Total Refunds	**0**	**$0.00**	**$0.00**
TOTAL REFERRAL FEES	14	$297.48	$18.48

amazon.com

Amazon, Amazon.com and the Amazon.com logo are registered
trademarks of Amazon.com, Inc. or its affiliates.

Web Site Tracking for Associates

Amazon also offers Web tracking IDs, where Associates can analyze the performance results of various Web sites or merchandising strategies at the same time as acquiring their earnings under
a single Associates ID. For instance, one Associate might use the
tracking ID to follow referrals from a Web site and other referrals
from the blog. Then the Associate can view earnings for all tracking IDs together, or generate reports for each tracking ID separately. You can create tracking IDs for your Associates account by
clicking on "Manage your Tracking ID" link. With the features
available here, you will be able to analyze your performance and
build custom links. This will help you:

- **Get faster results**. The information is easy to read and
  fast to load.

- **Measure performance expediently.** Reports data for
  Associates accounts, including the tracking ID for
  each transaction. Acquire all the data required in a

single download instead of generating a report for each tracking ID.

- **Save time while building links**. You can change the tracking ID to be used in the resulting code at any time while you are building links. This increases your flexibility and eliminates the need for you to repeat steps.

CHAPTER 16

MP3 and the Kindle Offer New Horizons

Amazon is continually developing and introducing new products. Naturally, this is ideal for Amazon Associates Program members, as they will be able to sell these new items — frequently at a higher commission percentage.

Introducing the Amazon MP3

Amazon opened a new MP3 store that does not have digital rights management (DRM) software, so Amazon MP3 users can freely get music downloads with any hardware device, arrange their songs with an application for music management, and burn songs to CDs.

Among the DRM-free titles available is the record company EMI Group, which offers music without copy protection. EMI, which claims to offer the most extensive selection of separate, DRM-free MP3 music downloads, joined 12,000 smaller, independent music companies that chose not to use the copy-restricting software. With more than two million songs from more than 180,000 artists that are supported by 20,000-plus leading and secondary labels, Amazon MP3 matches Amazon's current choice of more than one million CDs to provide users greater selection of physical and digital music than any other retailer.

Each Amazon MP3 song and album is available solely in the MP3 format. The majority of songs cost $0.89 to $0.99, with more than half of the two million songs at $0.89. The majority of albums cost $5.99 to $9.99, with most leading, popular albums priced at $8.99. All songs are encoded at 256 kilobits per second, offering high audio quality at an easy-to-manage file size. All sales gained through the widget earn Associates 10 percent of the sale.

CASE STUDY: MANUEL BURGOS

Manuel Burgos
Rare Arts
640 Belmont Avenue
Brooklyn, NY 11207
(718) 554-3869
www.rarearts.com

Manuel (Manny) Burgos pursued his background in illustration from 1981 and started his Brooklyn graphics firm, Rare Arts, in 1999, particularly to meet the unique needs of small businesses and political candidates in New York City. One of the highlights of the company was developing the logo and design elements for the campaign of William Thompson, NYC Comptroller. The firm also custom designs maps and restores photographs.

This year, Burgos entered the publishing field, with two books written specifically for and about Amazon's Kindle: *Graphics on the Kindle* and *Formatting Comics for the Kindle.* Future books will cover illustrations for children's literature and cooking.

A drawback of the Kindle has been the quality of the graphics. Burgos' books move this negative more into the plus side.

"I fell in love with the Kindle as soon as I saw it," Burgos said. "Every year, I am putting up new book shelves in my house, and I'm running out of room. Now I can have thousands of books to read and not take up any space."

CASE STUDY: MANUEL BURGOS

The publishing arm of Rare Arts helps writers looking to bypass the publishing houses and enter the world of electronic books. It lays out e-books and prepares them for a variety of e-book readers, including the Amazon Kindle.

Rare Arts consists of six designers, Web developers, writers, photographers, and videographers. Said Burgos, "We give each project our full attention and always meet or exceed customer deadlines. Our motto, 'If you're working, we're working!,' is our way of saying that we respect how hard our customers work and understand the unusual hours a small business has to keep to stay running (especially a home-based business)."

Introducing the Amazon Kindle

amazon.com

Amazon, Amazon.com and the Amazon.com logo are registered trademarks of Amazon.com, Inc. or its affiliates.

Another new product by Amazon is "Kindle," which, in typical Amazon tradition, represents a daring move for an "online bookstore." Amazon intentionally decided to develop and create a completely new type of device — an easy-to-use-and-carry reading tool with the ability to electronically download all forms of reading materials, from books to blogs. Amazon introduced Kindle to offer a high-quality reading experience.

Because of the high-grade electronic paper, the screen is just like reading a typical book or newspaper — there is no eyestrain or glare. It works using ink, just like books and newspapers, but shows the ink particles electronically and uses no backlighting, which eliminates the glare associated with other electronic displays. It can be read in all forms of lighting, from bright sunlight to low-lit rooms. Kindle is also very easy to use. It never gets hot no matter how long it is on, and can be operated without any difficulty by both right- and left-handed individuals.

To make it a totally portable unit, the wireless Kindle needs no PC and syncing. Working on the 3G network as do cell phones, the Kindle relies on Whispernet®, Amazon's wireless system. Contrary to Wi-Fi systems, the readers never need to find a hotspot. In addition, readers do not have to be concerned about paying monthly bills, annual contracts, or service plans. They can just download one of the thousands of books and instantly start reading regardless of where you are located, be it at home, work, or on the train. It is also very light, as it takes the place of heavy books to carry around. The small size and huge memory allows readers to easily carry a whole library with them. Nearly any book readers have ever wanted is easily on hand.

Kindle has the most sizeable book selection by far, with more than 120,000 books, magazines, newspapers, and blogs, including 98 of 112 current *New York Times* Best Sellers). Once one book is finished in a series, it is on to the next. If the reader is not sure if he or she will like a book, it is possible to download it for free and read an excerpt. If the readers like the book, they can simply acquire it with one click and continue reading. Readers can also wake up in the morning and get a wirelessly delivered newspaper, even before most papers are sent to the newsstands. All subscriptions begin with a two-week trial period.

It is expected that the Kindle will bring in between $400 and $750 million in revenue by 2010, or 1 to 3 percent of Amazon's total revenue. Kindle is not limited to books that Amazon sells — it can read books in Mobipocket or text formats and also Audible. com^{SM}'s protected audio books, HTML and Word documents, and several image formats (through Amazon's e-mail-based conversion service). It includes extremely limited MP3 music support as well. Kindle has more memory than those by the competitors and supports newspapers, magazines, and blog subscriptions.

CASE STUDY: STEPHEN WINDWALKER

Stephen Windwalker
Harvard Perspectives Press
P.O. Box 400827
Cambridge, MA 02140
http://indiekindle.blogspot.com

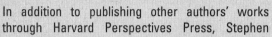

In addition to publishing other authors' works through Harvard Perspectives Press, Stephen Windwalker started writing and publishing his own books and marketing them through Amazon. He began with *Selling Used Books Online* in 2002 because of his past experience as a bookseller.

When the Kindle was introduced, Windwalker was another immediate fan. As an Amazon Associate, he began selling Kindles, and in 2008 published another book, *Beyond the Literary-Industrial Complex: How Authors and Publishers Are Using the Amazon Kindle and Other New Technologies to Unleash a 21st-Century Indie Movement of Readers & Writers*. From the start, Windwalker saw Kindle as a perfect vehicle for emerging, independent, and self-published authors to beta test or introduce their books — either in completed form or as excerpts.

He practiced what he preached and, while completing his own book on Kindle, excerpted chapters as freestanding articles for Kindle readers. His readership quickly mounted to the Kindle bestseller list. He had more than 1,400 readers in the first couple of weeks and, a few months later, had sold 20,000 "copies" of his work.

Not thinking that his downloads would rise this fast, Windwalker promised his 10-year-old son his own Kindle once there were 8,000 downloads. Needless to say, his son has his own Kindle now.

CASE STUDY: STEPHEN WINDWALKER

Windwalker understands how to take advantage of Amazon marketing opportunities. He has two blogs that promote the Kindle, is an Amazon affiliate, and sells his own books through Amazon. He said that Amazon has a very strong search infrastructure that has helped promote his sites.

He emphasized that anyone who wants to sell a book to be read on a Kindle can do that now, by promoting the content as a text file download, or by selling it as a text file on a CD. In addition, there is a great deal of free literary content available through Kindle.

The Kindle's Variety of Advantages

- **High readability:** A paper-like display (167 dpi, four-level grayscale) is featured along with a custom, anti-aliased typeface with six sharp and clear text sizes.

- **Impact resistant:** The plastic exterior with a case flexes and absorbs impact when dropped.

- **Unique controls:** A scroll/click wheel and accessible buttons and a compact keyboard are located at the bottom on the face front. Volume buttons are on the bottom edge, and the power and wireless switches are on the back near the top.

- **Menu navigation:** Menus and text selection are controlled by a scroll wheel running up and down the right-hand side of the display. Just rotate the wheel up the side of the screen next to the object that needs to be manipulated, then click the wheel to choose menu options and document and text hyperlinks.

- **Resource guide:** Readers can look up words in the enclosed Oxford American Dictionary, select high-lighted texts, or use the keyboard to add notes for text selection.

- **Accessibility plus:** Later, if you want to find the notes that you made, just use the "My Clippings." This infor-mation also can be found as a text file in order to copy to a Mac or PC.

- **Popular buttons:** On the left hand side of the page, you can find the Previous Page and Next Page buttons.

- **Backward look:** If you would like to go back to the pre-vious place in your document, just use the back button. Readers like this feature because it helps them when perusing through other written materials, such as mag-azines, blogs, and newsletters

- **Accessible keyboard:** You can easily access the keyboard. It is located at the bottom third of the Kindle face.

- **Volume control:** Located at the bottom of the unit are volume control buttons, as well as a standard 3.5 mm stereo headphone jack, mini-B USB connector, and AC adapter and battery charger power connector.

- **Playing MP3s:** You can multitask whenever you want. Enjoy music tracks while reading.

- **Protective cover:** The safety of your unit is also a major consideration. The rubber plate on the back can be easily removed to get to the batteries, digital memory card slot, and pinhole reset switch.

- **Battery recharge:** You can read for approximately two days' worth of reading with the wireless and the battery. Then, just recharge the unit in two hours with the AC adapter.

- **Wide selection of content:** There is never a loss for something to read. You can download Amazon and non-Amazon copy, as the Kindle also works with the Mobipocket format and provides scores of eBooks from numerous other publishers. For little to no money, you can have a lot of good content.

- **Communication features:** If you need to send messages, the Kindle's e-mail-based service accepts Microsoft Word, HTML, prc, mobi, and text files, as well as jpeg, gif, png, and bmp image files. For just 10 cents, Amazon wirelessly sends the converted document to the Kindle and makes it a snap to connect to a Mac or PC.

- **Publishing ease:** For your business, consider using a Kindle to sell e-books. This is a perfect way to sell your subject-area expertise and make incremental income. It only takes a few minutes to get the e-book up and running.

- **Author perks:** Once your book is on Amazon, you can decide what you would like to charge. Set the price from 99 cents to $200 and get 35 percent of each sale. Amazon uses sales and promotions, but does not reduce your royalties and allows you to set the price that you feel is will be most profitable.

- **Digital text platform:** You can even reach more potential readers and buyers through Amazon's large readership environment numbers, which are growing every day.

- **High potential:** There are already two Kindle versions, so expect more with additional features that will help promote your business.

- **Long readership:** Once someone invests in the Kindle, you can expect that this reader will be greatly used for a long time. Kindle is not going to replace books, but it does give avid readers another way to get their fix of prose and information.

Associates Site Stripe

Amazon always has something new in store for its Associates. The latest offering is called Site Stripe, which allows affiliates to create links directly from the Amazon site without having to visit Associates Central. You can build links to any page on Amazon and even add products to your aStore. It also has handy shortcuts to some other useful Associates pages. Associates say this is another time saver from Amazon. The new quick linking feature is especially useful because it should save a great deal of time when Associates link to specific products. Previously, if Associates wanted to insert a relevant link into one of their articles — for example a link to a another page — they had to log into their Amazon account, use the search engine to find the specific title, and navigate through a series of options just to find the correct HTML text to paste into the article. Now, all they need to do is go to the desired product page, click on the "Link to this page" option from the site stripe, and the HTML code for the affiliate link is automatically generated. There are four buttons available on the Site Stripe: 1) The "Link to this page" noted above; 2) "Adding to aStore," where product can easily be added to the aStore; 3) "Your Earnings Report," for a quick short-cut to earnings; and 4) "Settings" for configuring the Site Stripe.

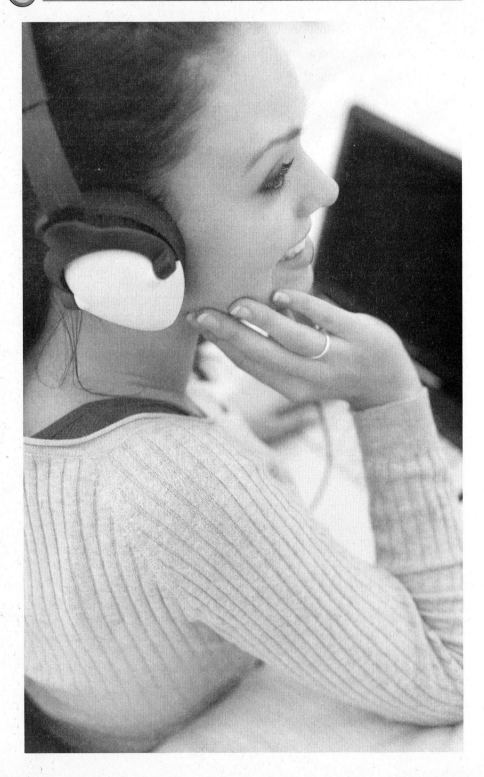

CHAPTER 17

Best Reasons for Becoming an Associate

Every day, new people are joining the Amazon Associates program. Some use it in conjunction with their blog as a lucrative way to gain an extra benefit from the people who come to their Web site to learn about a specific topic. Some add several Amazon products to their own merchandising mix to have an extra advantage from Amazon's brand and their own unique items. Others build an aStore and have no need to be concerned about any of their own inventory. Many Associates have multiple blogs, Web sites, or uses for Amazon in social sites. These Associates know that with the right amount of personal effort and commitment, this decision can be a beneficial way to earn supplementary income. These are some of the main benefits of the Associates Program:

- **Amazon's branding:** Amazon has become a household word. People all over the world are familiar with Amazon, even if they only know that it is a major online store or that it is associated with books. It is a positive and well-known brand. In surveys, Amazon is one of the top recognized Web names or companies where online buyers purchase products. Organizations spend many years and significant resources to develop a brand. With the Associates program, you can rely on the expert branding that Amazon has accomplished to instill trust and credibility in your business among your customers.

- **Generating incremental income:** If someone accepts a sales position where part or all of the salary is based on commission, it is understood that this will take diligence, patience, strategy, and commitment, though this person also knows that the more effort put into the position, the more that will be financially gained. It is similar with Amazon. One has to look beyond the 4 or 6 percent commission per item, which is only going to bring in a dollar here or there on smaller items. It is important to look beyond that scenario and see what the commission is going to be on multiple or larger items. There are Associates who bring in small amounts of money, but these are the ones who would not do well with a sales position. There also are those who make thousands of dollars a month. There is a reason why some people are successful nine-to-fivers, and some people are successful entrepreneurs. Neither of these is right or wrong; each person has different goals and interests in life. It does take a certain type of person to become an Amazon Associates Program member, and that person can do quite well financially.

- **The more the merrier:** Have you ever gone into a store for one specific item and then left with many in your hands? How many times do people go into a bookstore for one book and come out with several? When someone clicks on an Amazon link on an Associate's Web site for one item of interest, there is a good chance that this person will be buying more than just that one book or pet product. You get commissions on all the additional merchandise purchased within 24 hours as well.

- **It is so easy:** All you have to do is sign up and spend an hour of your time integrating the Amazon tools into your own Web site or using Amazon products entirely; it is a no-brainer. Yes, once you set up the business, it does take work to bring customers to your site, but that is always the case with any business. Still, try to go out and build a brick-and-mortar business or establish a new online presence in this short of time. Impossible.

- **Here a widget, there a widget:** Once you have the Web site, then you can customize it in any way that you want. There are so many different permutations, links, and widgets available that you can have a field day trying all the various ways to integrate Amazon's tools: A carousel of products swinging around, music that plays, videos that show, windows that open, splashes of color, borders, and banners. Online visitors like change. They also like clarity and order. Both of these are available with Amazon.

- **Special prizes:** Blog experts and merchandisers know that one of the ways to entice people to come to their Web site, or stay to on it, is to offer prizes or specials. You can use your Amazon gift certificates or products for giveaways. How about those few dollars you received from the commission? You can have that paid as a product and give it back to build your customer list or blog readership.

- **Something is better than nothing:** Let us say you only make a few dollars the first several months of becoming an Associate because perhaps you have not had a great deal of time to spend on this enterprise, or you are still trying to find the right product mix or promotional approach to bring in customers. What have you lost? You still are on the plus side. Remember, patience is one of the most important words when you are working online with Amazon or any affiliate or Web site. It takes time to get action and reaction with those millions of people who are going online every day. A few bucks in your pocket will add up and have the possibility of building up well over time.

- **Gaining from knowledge:** If you start a new business that you know nothing about, it is going to take time for you to learn the ins and outs. It is no different with becoming an Amazon Associate. Over time, you will find the tricks that will work and those that are duds. You will find how to open more doors of earnings with Amazon, either because that opportunity was there all along and you did not know it, or Amazon just added a new bell or whistle. One thing that is true about Amazon is it is constantly transforming its business.

- **Cashing in on promotions:** The people at Amazon are not sitting around and waiting for the money to come in. They are also looking for new ways to add to their bottom line. There are all those specials they have on products, which you can also advertise. Also, as any merchandiser knows, you can use hooks for promoting certain products during the year. The reason why Mother's Day, Secretary's Day, and Sweetest Day are celebrated is because the card companies promote them. How can you use Amazon products best on Valentine's Day, Father's Day, or that wonderful end-of-the-year holiday time? You have to always be looking into the future when you are running a business. That is why spring clothes are in the stores way before the end of winter.

- **Thousands and thousands of products:** The interesting thing about people is that they all share certain interests, but, on the other hand, they all have their particular unique interests. Just look at what people collect. Some may collect antique toys, but others may collect bottle caps or even hubcaps. You never know what people are going to want to buy, and you cannot be all things to all people. Actually, most e-commerce and blog experts know that finding a niche area of interest is the best route to take with a Web site. With millions and millions of people going online every day, even a small percentage of them looking for bottle caps is a large number.

Competing in today's online world is complex. In the e-commerce world, providing a friendly and supportive site for a specific population can be an incredibly successful strategy. Analysts say that although there are the big sites such as Amazon online, there still is a place in cyberspace for the niche sites. As an Amazon Associate, you can have your cake and eat it, too. You can be a niche and be part of that larger e-commerce world of "the Amazons."

The smaller businesses that have the best chance of succeeding online, according to these financial analysts, are those who can build brand awareness and provide goods that buyers are not able to find anyplace else, or have difficulty finding elsewhere. Do some traveling online and look around at the businesses and bloggers who have chosen this route of specialization. Amazon has so many different products that you are bound to find something that will pertain to these specialized buyers coming to your Web site.

Tips of the Trade

In another chapter, this book will cover some of the ways that you can promote your business. For now, though, here are some things to remember when running your business using Amazon Associates.

As noted above, people more often than not have a specific interest. As the saying goes, you are never going to please all of the people all of the time. Yet, you can please some of the people some of the time. Always give thought to what your customers, readers, music listeners, or video watchers want. Actually, you should be one of those people as well, since it is best to sell or writing about your own interests. It is not even necessary to put yourself in their shoes, as you are already wearing them. What products do you like? What makes you buy? What will bring someone else like you to your Web site and on Amazon?

Reputation, as Amazon knows, truly counts. You need to spread the word about your Web site, and that can be done with those visitors who have become regulars. They will tell others either through conventional ways or through testimonials on your site. Think back to those rating stars that measure different aspects of products and merchandisers on Amazon. There is a reason for these ratings: People will buy from and go to sites that have proven positive experiences. To build a positive reputation and have people returning to your Web site or blog, you have to be honest and let others know why you feel pros and cons about issues and products from your perspective. That is why they should be coming to your site: Because they know they can get a well-rounded idea about something before they invest their money.

You are offering them your expertise and knowledge about whatever product or service that you provide on your Web site. They do not want to hear that every product is wonderful; they want to know why it is wonderful for everyone, why it is only wonderful for some people, or why it is not wonderful for anyone. They respect your input is long as it is truthful.

That is also why anything you recommend, be it a product or another Web site, has to be high-quality as well. You surely do not want to suggest that people buy a product that is known to have major problems or falls apart the first time it is washed, nor do you want to send them to another Web site for additional information when it is erroneous. Something may look good for you in the short term — an extra bonus for adding a link to your Web site — but in the long run, you may lose visitors.

Amazon has a long and extensive following, but you need to work on that following. Too many people go online and think all they have to do is put up a banner, but throwing a banner here or a there haphazardly is not going to sell. You need to get into the heads of your visitors or blog readers and know what is relevant to them. This is why the copy on your page is so important; it needs to be completely integrated with the product you are selling.

If you have a Web site store or blog that sells bed and bath items and are writing about a new product that you endorse, this is where that text widget goes. As their mouse goes over the words, "new product," the window pops up from Amazon, showing the photo and price of that item. If you have specialized in offering tips to men and women who do a significant amount of traveling in their jobs, the Amazon Kindle widget can easily be placed in convenient, rational locations. This is not to say that your site should be covered with links; remember that order and clarity are just as important to that visitor.

Also take note of standard tried-and-true advertising. How do people read in your country? In the United States, most people read from far left down, so that upper, far-left corner is going to be seen a lot. What are you going to put there that pertains to most of the people who look at your site? How often should you change it? Or, can it be something from Amazon that changes on its own?

What other areas of your site are going to attract attention? If you have a special prize being given away, you can bet that your visitors' eyes will be moving that way. What item of interest will you be placing near that giveaway? Most likely, it should be something that is extremely close to what is being won in the drawing. You know that the people who sign up for the drawing want that product, so what better place to advertise an item that is in that same family of merchandise?

When those people sign up for a free gift, e-mail questions or comments, or purchase a product on your site, you are building a list to increase your traffic; that list is vital. Keep it growing. You need to continuously build your relationship with the people who are interested in your Web site. These will be the people who will buy again and tell others to buy through you.

Niches are important. Because Amazon allows 100 different sites, you can have a number of different niches that are of interest to you and others like you. This way, you are not just relying on one Web site to bring in all your business. You have several bringing in income at the same time. But do not overdo it. You do not want to get yourself so muddled that your sites become watered down. Just take note that you do not have to base everything you do on just one Web site or blog. Actually, if you keep these Web sites in some broad area of interest, you can link back and forth and have interested people going from one to the other.

Also recall that Amazon will let you know what your potential buyers were purchasing through Amazon after they left your Web site. This will give you an idea of some possible ways that you can expand your product line without going too far in another field.

Always remember that you have a two-fold objective. The first is to bring people to your Web site and keep them there — and coming back for more. The second is to continually open up avenues for them to want to go to Amazon and actually do so. You will see your sales steadily increase as you closely incorporate the theme of your site along with Amazon products that specifically fit the topic. You do not want to only provide information, nor do you just want to push products at people. Neither of these will make you successful in business. There is a fine balance here, and you will find it with time.

This is why it is so important to have information in addition to products. Even if you have an aStore, you can include valuable and interesting information for your visitors. This keeps them coming back; this builds your reputation; this sells products. Amazon products can also be picked up by the search engines and bring more people to your site.

Always make the best of the daily records that Amazon sends you. These are worth quite a bundle by themselves. They can tell you a lot about your customers — what makes them buy, what makes them stay or leave, what makes them like your site or not. Keep meticulous notes on how and when you change your Web site, so you can track the impact on your visitors. When you added a certain widget, changed the location of the ads, or tried a new technique, what happened? Is this something that you should continue or not?

Do not forget all the other successful Amazon Associates out there who can lend you advice. Through forums, e-mail, and even phone calls, you can find out why another Associate does or does not do something on a Web site — or if you should try a certain approach. It almost certainly has been done by someone else who can provide insight even before you try it. There is a wealth of information online from your fellow Associates. If you see something that interests you, do not hesitate to get in touch with that other affiliate.

Most importantly, always think outside of the box. That is what Amazon has been doing for a decade, and that is what you should be doing as well. Status quo never works in this day and age. Thinking inside the box means accepting that everything is fine just the way it is. If Jeff Bezos had thought that way, Amazon would never have existed.

In-the-box thinkers are just what the image implies. They are caught in a box; every way that they turn, they are surrounded by walls and obstacles. They cannot find their way out of the box and see anything beyond these four walls. They find it especially difficult to realize that they can come up with new ideas, let alone begin thinking about them. When someone tries to give them a new way to approach a situation or a different way to improve an ongoing, or even a struggling, program, they put up their blinders and put in their ear plugs. They make innovative people who are thinking with imagination feel worthless.

These people say, "This is the way things have been done, and this is the way they will continue to be done." They love shooting down anything new; it is too scary and way too risky. "This one solution has worked for a long time, so it will continue to work for a long time to come. Why is an alternative needed? This one works fine. Let's not muddy up the waters with another option." Not only are these "in-the-box" thoughts unhealthy in the real world; in the e-commerce virtual world, they are deadly.

Thinking out of the box is being innovative, creative, and even crazy at times. That is what many people thought about Bezos and Amazon. The term "outside the box" is believed to come from the known puzzle developed by British mathematician Henry Ernest Dudeney, who lived in the early 20th century. In this test, people are asked to only draw four straight lines without the pen leaving the paper, in order to interconnect nine dots in a three-by-three grid without the pen leaving the paper. To be successful, the puzzle solver has to realize that he or she has to go beyond normally considered boundaries. The puzzle can only be solved in one way, or extending the lines further than the artificial boundary created by the nine dots.

Thinking outside the box means:

- A willingness, actually an eagerness, to want to go outside the boundaries and see what else is available.

- A desire to stretch one's capabilities and learn something new every day.

- The ability to say no to status quo, no matter how successful it has been in the past.

- Being able to accept other far-out, yet very possible, ideas from others.

- Spending part of each and every day thinking about new ways to approach old problems and reading what others have to say.

- Understanding that the cyber world is exceptionally different from the real world. It is in constant flux and is made up of people who cover every different interest imaginable.

- Accepting that some of the innovative ideas are not going to work, and going back to your brain power and trying another approach.

Is the Amazon Associates Program Best for You?

This is impossible to answer here for everyone. Nothing is perfect for all people, even those who are online pros. Yet, there are a good number of Associates who make a flow of money either through their own businesses with added Amazon products, blogs, sold Amazon merchandise, or aStores. It is necessary to keep that concept of niche and associated products, integrate with Amazon on a regular basis, attract and retain visitors, and most importantly, enjoy what you do.

CASE STUDY: SHAWN COLLINS

Shawn Collins
Shawn Collins Consulting
221 Sherman Ave
Ste #8 PMB 185
Berkeley Heights, NJ 07922-1173
(908) 364-2767
http://blog.affiliatetip.com

After working in the magazine publishing field with Ziff Publishing, Shawn Collins jumped into the Internet, with what is now **www.Medsite.com** and CafeMom (**www.CafeMom.com**). His involvement as an Amazon Associate goes back to 1997. He is the author of *Successful Affiliate Marketing for Merchants* and co-founder of the Affiliate Summit with Missy Ward in 2003 "for the purpose of providing educational sessions on the latest industry issues and fostering a productive networking environment for affiliate marketers." He publishes the annual *AffStatReport*, which includes research, analysis, and benchmarking information for the affiliate marketing industry.

Collins calls Amazon a leader in affiliate marketing, not only because it was one of the first to introduce the affiliate concept, but also due to having "the most options and advantages" for its affiliates. For example, he highly rates the addition of widgets to the Amazon Web site structure. This is just an example of how Amazon is continually updating its affiliate offerings.

Collins also gives a thumbs-up to Amazon's in-house product opportunities. "They literally sell everything I want to sell. It's a gigantic inventory that can be very lucrative as substantial incremental income."

The biggest mistake by affiliates, he said, is a "lack of investment and understanding. It's very difficult to be a success in affiliate marketing if you are un-

CASE STUDY: SHAWN COLLINS

willing to spend the time and money required to develop a long-term strategy. Affiliate marketing is definitely not a quick endeavor; it takes patience to endure and succeed."

 **CHAPTER 18**

Amazon's High-Tech Web Services

The Amazon Associates Web Services is a part of the business that gives the company product data exposure with the use of a convenient interface that gives Web site developers, owners, and merchants the opportunity to grow their income. Developers use the Amazon Associates Web Services to drive visitors to Amazon to purchase products or services.

This gives them an effective way to create robust and considerably effectual applications that merchandises sellers' goods. You can have free access to Web Services if you want to leverage it for selling, reselling, redistributing, sublicensing, or transferring the data, but need to receive written consent in advance. Web services, similarly, can be used with permission for use with any handheld, mobile, or mobile phone application. To receive commissions when selling Amazon products, it is necessary to sign-up with Amazon Associates and make sure your links that are made with the Web Services accurately contain your Associate's tag. You only pay for those services that you use.

With Web Services, developers can earn extra income and build traffic with:

- **Amazon Elastic Compute Cloud (EC2®)** that makes Web-scale computing easier for developers. Use this option to alter server capacity in just minutes; have a wide choice of operating systems and software packages; work with other Amazon services for computing, query processing and storage across a myriad of applications; and interface for firewall setting configuration.

- **Amazon SimpleDB** that provides the main database operations of data indexing and querying. It works closely with Amazon Simple Storage Service (Amazon S3) and Amazon EC2 to collectively offer the capability to stock, process, and query data sets in the cloud, making Web-scale computing simpler and more cost-efficient.

- **Amazon S3** that offers an easy-to-use Web interface for storage and retrieval for any amount of data and any time Web-wide. Developers can access the same highly scalable and robust data storage infrastructure that Amazon relies on to operate its own Web sites. It optimizes benefits of scale and gives those advantages to developers.

- **Amazon CloudFront™** that provides high-quality service for content delivery. It gives developers and merchants an effective means to integrate with other Web Services to offer content to end users with high-data transfer speeds.

- **Amazon Simple Queue Service (Amazon SQS)** provides a dependable hosted queue to store messages traveling among computers. With Amazon SQS, developers can just transfer data among application components that complete various tasks and not lose messages, or need every component to always be usable. This service optimizes the convenience to build an automated workflow and work in tandem with Amazon EC2 and Web Services features.

- **Amazon Elastic Map Reduce** allows developers, businesses, analysts, and researchers to readily and cost-efficiently process large quantities of data. It uses a hosted Hadoop framework working on the Amazon EC2 Amazon S3 and infrastructures.

By using Web Services, you can increase your earnings, as your visitors are enticed by even more in-depth product information. Amazon has spent more than a decade and $2 billion building this Web Services computing platform.

CASE STUDY: RICHARD GELLER, CEO

Richard Geller, CEO
www.DesiredResultsMarketing.org
Fairfax, Virginia
703-637-9163

Through his company, **www.DesiredResultsMar-keting.org**, Richard Geller helps local advertisers gain more business on the Web. He has been involved with various Web ventures since the earliest days online and is continuously looking for additional ways to streamline his business and reduce costs and resources.

"I've been very pleased with the Amazon S3 Web Services," Geller said. Amazon S3 provides a simple Web Services interface for storage and retrieval of any amount of data, at any time, from anywhere on the Web. It gives developers access to the same highly scalable, reliable, and fast data storage infrastructure that Amazon uses to run its own global network of Web sites.

"Before using Amazon, I relied on my ISP to store and retrieve my clients' video and audio files for Web sites and blogs," said Geller. "However, since the bandwidth was so high, this approach worked too slowly." Geller said that with Amazon Web Services, there can be a million files being down- or uploaded at a time, and there is no problem with speed.

Geller also plans on using the Amazon fulfillment center in the near future for some of his promotional books and tapes. "As soon as an order comes in, the product goes out... sometimes as quick as a four-hour turnaround time. I could never do this on my own."

CHAPTER 19

Private Branding with Amazon's WebStore

Amazon's WebStore allows you to:

- Create your own branded e-commerce site in minutes.

- Customize a Web site that suits your own merchandise theme and style and that can easily be updated and previewed.

- Open a store with your own name and brand. You use your own domain name and URL address, and not a sub-domain off the main URL.

- Have multiple WebStores under a single account with unlimited number of transactions, with no additional monthly fees.

- Have an easy way to manage your site. It is simple to create and manage your product inventory, descriptions, images, and orders from your home-office location.

- Use Amazon's marketing tools to get you started on your venture. You can successfully promote your merchandise by adding product recommendations, customer reviews, and recently viewed items.

- Offer an e-commerce site backed by Amazon's A-to-z Guarantee.

- Gain the use of both the WebStore and Amazon Associates account at the same time. You can promote items in your WebStore that you are marketing as an Associate, and they show right next to your other product line.

Have you thought for a long time about starting your own branded online store, but have been putting it off because you are afraid that you do not have the time, resources, or skills? Put aside your reluctance and fears. With Amazon's WebStore, you can create your own e-commerce Web site using Amazon's technology, sales channel, marketing tools, purchasing, search mode, merchandising, invoicing, and fulfillment services. If you would like to easily build a Web site and enhance your product visibility, as well as make it easier for your customers to buy online, track their orders, and enjoy Amazon's shipping perks, this is the best solution for you.

Briefly, the WebStore is a product that gives you the opportunity to build and maintain a tailored, branded e-commerce site and sell your own products. At the same time, you can leverage the

Amazon technology, so you can have a total, packaged solution to online success. You get more than a WebStore when you sign up with Amazon; you also receive a personal domain Web site that allows you to tap into all the technical advantages that Amazon has been crafting for years. With the feature called "Seller Central," you can completely design and maintain your WebStore right from your computer. You can add or alter information on products or services, enhance inventory, pick up your new orders, and make your Web site design even more appealing. For increased marketing purposes, your products will be listed both on your Web Site and on Amazon itself.

Amazon also gives your customers the opportunity to leave reviews and/or feedback on your products or services. If you get positive reviews from your customers for everyone to see, it is free advertising. When you go into your account, all you need to do is click on "Seller Performance" to see your latest reviews.

Easy-to-Build Site with Added Customer Protection

Another popular Amazon feature is called 1-Click WebStore. With just one click of your mouse, you can construct your WebStore. After signing up with Amazon, you can easily use this 1-Click feature to make your Web Site look and feel the way you want. There are several templates from which to choose, along with their unique colors and design. If you would rather have something more unique than these templates, you can quickly design your own page with Amazon's tools. Once you feel that you have everything up and ready to view by your customers, check it out before going live with the simple publish-and-preview feature. At this point, you should look at the amount of time it takes to download the graphics. You do not want your customers to get impatient and go to another site because it took too long to get on your site. There are enough widgets and visuals from which to choose that you can find a happy medium between a dynamic design and the download time.

Adding your inventory to the WebStore is just as easy as the design with the Amazon tools, downloading software application, or flat files. If one of your items is discontinued, out of stock, or not available when you are published online, you will see a hole in your category page. When you take out this product or offer it for sale, you will need to publish your WebStore again in order to finalize the changes. Your customers will use their Amazon customer account to add products to their shopping cart and purchase them. People without these accounts can easily create one when they are ready to shop. Meanwhile, anyone who buys under the Amazon name receives the company's safety protection. To manage your orders, it is just as easy as the design and sale. You receive a notice through your e-mail or through Seller Central when a customer orders. If necessary, you can use this same online tool to keep track of all orders, as well as give customer refunds.

Plus, when you start your business, you need to have more than just products. You also need some means of protecting yourself as well as your customers. Amazon protects you from payment fraud and makes sure that customer orders are legitimate. Further, the company covers you with the A-to-z Guarantee. Both you and your customers can feel comfortable knowing that the purchased items are being protected.

Fulfillment Services Available for WebStore

Similar to other Amazon programs, the WebStore owners can use Amazon's fulfillment services and spend time building the business — and not packing and sending. Your inventory and orders are processed utilizing the same system used by Amazon, which handles all the picking, packing, and shipping well before the expected mail date. After a decade of business and millions of orders, Amazon's fulfillment center has evolved into one of the most advanced networks. Fulfillment by Amazon (FBA) can be used for Amazon orders or those from other channels, your own Web site, or catalog and in-store retail sales. You always own and control your FBA inventory and can send more, or request returns at any time. Fulfillment fees are charged to you at the time of a sale, and FBA items are eligible for Super Saver Shipping and Amazon Prime.

With Amazon Drop Ship, you can procure millions of products from multiple suppliers in addition to Amazon and re-sell them to your customers while maintaining no inventory or warehouse. You can place orders for products listed on the Amazon Web site using Drop Ship by Amazon, and the merchandise is shipped directly to your customers. You can also benefit from the wide selection of products in more than 40 categories at extremely competitive prices. With Drop Ship by Amazon, you can sell millions of products to customers without needing to stock or pre-purchase anything; customize your product selection and display the merchandise on your Web site; leverage a broad, deep product selection based on the Amazon Web site listings and extensive fulfillment capabilities with Amazon Web Services; and determine the prices you charge your customers.

CASE STUDY: LARRY & DOTTIE NYLIN

Larry and Dottie Nylin
In the Garden and More
1218 Clarendon Street
Durham, NC 27705
919-286-3623
www.inthegardenandmore.com

Larry and Dottie Nylin are ministers who work with
those in need in the Raleigh/Durham, North Carolina area. In 2001, they began their Web business, "In the Garden and More," which sells garden décor for outdoor and indoor living, as a means to support themselves as they ventured into full-time ministry. Their initial Web site was not an Amazon WebStore. In 2005, they were approached by Amazon WebStore, and they were so impressed with its ease of function that they closed their initial Web site and went totally with the Amazon WebStore. It has been a great advantage for them.

The WebStore is an ideal answer for the Nylins, because Amazon provides all the services they need: As the couple says, "WebStore by Amazon is simple to use, helps you create a Web site that has pizzazz and looks professional, and is easy to maintain. Plus, it also gives you two platforms on which to sell — Amazon.com, as well as your own WebStore — and they process all my credit card transactions. What could be better than that? WebStore by Amazon has been an excellent choice for our business. It is affordable and professional, and it has helped our business grow." Especially helpful, says Dottie Nylin, is the trust and the use of the Amazon name in search engine marketing.

Step-by-Step Instructions to Open Your Amazon WebStore

Before opening your WebStore, you will need to register and log in. The setup wizard guides you through a six-step process. You can create and manage your WebStore with Amazon's wizard and account management options. Merchants can register for the WebStore by visiting Amazon and clicking on the link at the bottom of the homepage and signing up: 1) with their existing Amazon Seller Community Account, 2) using their existing Amazon Customer Account, or 3) by creating a new Seller Account. Again, it is recommended that you use a separate account from your personal one.

1. When registering for their WebStore, sellers are asked to walk through a six-step process. Enter the business name as it should appear on the store.

2. Enter business address.

3. Enter credit card information.

4. Complete identity verification (by phone).

5. Review information.

6. Submit and log in to Seller Central.

WebStore provides a number of options to help merchants learn about this program and the process, including:

- WebStore Quick Start Guide
- WebStore Merchant Manual
- Contextual Help — Inline help on all the pages
- Seller Central Help Center Video Tutorial

Welcome to Amazon Services!
Please enter your login and password to access your Seller Central or Vendor Tools account. Need help

My e-mail address is:

My password is: Log In

amazon.com

Amazon, Amazon.com and the Amazon.com logo are registered trademarks of Amazon.com, Inc. or its affiliates.

You will be given an ID and password, or you can use the one that you already have. It is essential that you carefully read and approve the Amazon agreement. It is very easy to just click on "I agree" and keep on going, but there may be aspects of this agreement that you want to be aware of now rather than having to make changes later. You can use the scroll key to see the entire agreement. Also make a copy of this agreement and keep it in your files for future reference.

Once you agree to the terms and conditions on the first page of the Amazon Wizard, you can complete the application form with information about your company and soon be on your way as one of the next Amazon WebStore successes. You just need to fill in the blanks. The page will automatically fill in the fields you have just completed on the agreement page.

The information entered on this form will be readily visible to your customers. Furthermore, the company name you enter is used in the copyright information displayed in the footer, or the bottom, of each page of your store. Enter the exact name you want displayed in the footer. On this company information page, you may also want to upload an image of your company logo. Your customers will see this when they check out.

amazon.com

Amazon, Amazon.com and the Amazon.com logo are registered trademarks of Amazon.com, Inc. or its affiliates.

You get different choices to help you create a WebStore:

- Select a Theme. For example:

  The Natural theme offers: 1) Additional white space on the homepage, 2) a homepage element that spans the whole width of the page, which may either be a product image or Flash, 3) product information that may be placed below the image or Flash elements, 4) a menu bar that appears horizontally at the top of the homepage, and 5) a search box in the header.

  The WebStore Classic Theme offers: 1) A three-column design that allows the display of multiple images of products on your homepage, 2) a left column category menu bar that includes a search box, 3) space available in the menu bar for additional customized elements, 4) a center column to highlight the main attractions of the store, and 5) a right column that can accommodate a variety of page elements.

- **Choose a color**: With Amazon WebStore, you can choose a color from a variety of available choices. One is bound to characterize your Web site and your color interest. Each color scheme includes a thumbnail of the homepage, so you can preview how the design will look. You can always change your color scheme later; this selection just gets you started.

- **Select a style**: For example, blue style.

- **Provide store header image**: This is the name that will appear at the top of the WebStore. You will want to put in your own header and logo here.

- **Select products from inventory or add Amazon products**: Assign merchandise as either your own, unassigned, or Amazon Associate products, and place into categories; have the ability to search for products in any of these categories.

amazon.com

Amazon, Amazon.com and the Amazon.com logo are registered trademarks of Amazon.com, Inc. or its affiliates.

- Enter Associate ID to earn referral fees (optional).

- Get an on-screen progress bar with the status of your Web site creation. You can also have an e-mail sent to you when the process is complete.

- Be as creative as you would like to design your business' WebStore, with custom CSS (cascading style sheets), Flash, and many other preloaded text, image, audio and video widgets. It is a comprehensive template that is easy for designing various pages of your WebStore and adding custom tags and content to your Web site.

amazon.com

Amazon, Amazon.com and the Amazon.com logo are registered trademarks of Amazon.com, Inc. or its affiliates.

- Use keywords to enhance the optimization for search engines.

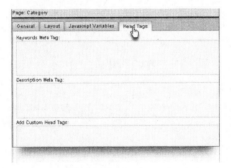

amazon.com

Amazon, Amazon.com and the Amazon.com logo are registered trademarks of Amazon.com, Inc. or its affiliates.

- Use the Export to Excel link to generate an Excel file with products.

- Add products to all your different WebStores with the Amazon Catalog, bulk uploads, and XML feeds.

amazon.com

Amazon, Amazon.com and the Amazon.com logo are registered trademarks of Amazon.com, Inc. or its affiliates.

• Utilize the Seller Central's Seller Desktop application Inventory Tab to find, edit, and delete products in your inventory.

• Publish all your updates to a preview or public domain name. By default, your domain will be **amazonWebstore.com**.

• Publish changes to existing items. Set the DNS and make changes in order to publish to a public domain.

• Take advantage of Amazon's sales and promotions.

amazon.com

Amazon, Amazon.com and the Amazon.com logo are registered trademarks of Amazon.com, Inc. or its affiliates.

- Order and generate multiple reports.

amazon.com

Amazon, Amazon.com and the Amazon.com logo are registered trademarks of Amazon.com, Inc. or its affiliates.

CASE STUDY: KATHY AND DAVE WOJTCZAK

Kathy and Dave Wojtczak

Element Jewelry and Accessories

www.elementjewelry.com

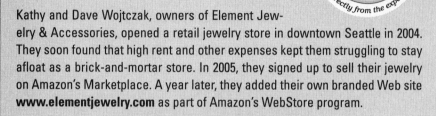

Kathy and Dave Wojtczak, owners of Element Jewelry & Accessories, opened a retail jewelry store in downtown Seattle in 2004. They soon found that high rent and other expenses kept them struggling to stay afloat as a brick-and-mortar store. In 2005, they signed up to sell their jewelry on Amazon's Marketplace. A year later, they added their own branded Web site **www.elementjewelry.com** as part of Amazon's WebStore program.

They had so much success selling on Amazon that when the store's lease was up in 2007, they decided to leave the world of physical retail behind. "Now, I manage our business from home. Customers can shop 24 hours a day, 365 days a year, while I have the freedom to work when I want from where I want," Kathy Wojtczak states. "I have been able to spend more time with my family, and even take a few vacations."

How does the couple sell in such a competitive category as jewelry? The answer is simple: They are able to keep their prices competitive because they no longer have the overhead and operating costs associated with selling in a physical store. "We are able to pass those savings on to our customers while still maintaining a good profit margin."

CASE STUDY: KATHY AND DAVE WOJTCZAK

That simple statement has actually changed every-thing. Before Kathy Wojtczak came to Amazon, her daily life was much different. "I worked in our store nine hours a day, six days a week, and 52 weeks a year. In-store traffic was unpredictable, advertis-ing was expensive, and store-related overhead was outrageous," she remembers. She was so busy

focusing on trying to keep her physical store growing that Amazon was not her main priority.

In June 2005, she uploaded about 100 items and started to watch the sales come in. She had two sales in June, so she added more inventory. She had 39 sales in September and kept going. In December, she had more than 200 sales. "Within six months, I knew that the growth potential from Amazon far exceeded the growth potential for my physical store," she said.

"My only regret is that I did not start selling on Amazon sooner," she said. She and Dave now offer more than 2,500 items on their Web site, and they are still growing. "This year our goal is to double our selection and double our sales from last year," the couple says. With the help of Amazon, it is possible for any business to follow in the Wojtczaks' footsteps and create its own success story, just as Kathy and Dave have.

CHAPTER 20

The Amazon Customer-Service Way

When you get your Amazon Associates or WebStore Web site up and running, you need to make sure it is getting the attention it requires, keeping visitors on the site longer, and having visitors return on a regular basis. Through your Amazon participation, you will receive the foundation for attention-getting and promotion for your products. It is up to you to build on that foundation to obtain optimal exposure for your merchandise. The Internet is a huge beast, and without spending time on marketing and promotion, a small e-commerce entity can be eaten up and may disappear.

Providing a Positive Buying Experience

Naturally, it is important to get new visitors to your Web site to buy products. Yet it is equally important to offer a positive buying experience, so they will want to purchase from you again.

Furthermore, you want your customers and potential buyers to enjoy coming to your Web site for more than just product viewing, and to remain on your site for some time before moving on.

Since it first started, Amazon placed a great deal of emphasis on customer service, and the company expects all its vendors to continue that tradition. Amazon offers several opportunities for customers to provide feedback on their recent purchases. The data provided by Amazon gives the sellers' rating over a period of time, up to a year. Consumers use the results of this feedback to decide which products to buy and from what vendors. Merchants need to maintain a high feedback score to remain competitive, especially in this present aggressive marketplace, and also to expect to retain their Amazon partnership.

If a buyer does not leave feedback after a sale, Amazon sends out a reminder of the order in 30 days. The consumer has up to 90 days to leave or remove feedback. Because this input is so important to future customers, you will want to encourage your buyers to comment on their experiences. Do not be afraid of getting responses. If you are running your business properly, the feedback will be positive. If you see negative feedback trends in a certain area — in packaging, for example — you will want to solve this problem as soon as possible. Amazon offers a list of best practices for sellers, based on the majority of negative comments it receives:

- **Inventory should be updated daily.** Customers are not pleased when they try to purchase an item and it is out of stock.

- **Pricing should be checked regularly.** To price your products, look at the cost of comparable products and make necessary changes. If a product has not sold for over a month, check your price to ensure that it remains competitive.

- **Send out your product no later than two business days of receiving the order.** Amazon requires this.

- **E-mail your buyer when you ship an item.** Let the customer know it is on the way and by what method it is being shipped.

- **Handle refunds and returns in a timely manner.** If you cannot fill an order, refund the amount within 48 hours, and send return refunds no later than five business days upon receiving.

- **Respond to all customer questions within 24 hours.** You will receive positive feedback when you communicate well with customers.

Here are some of the typical transaction problems:

- The item does not arrive, yet the customer is billed.

- The product is sent with flimsy or inadequate packaging and labeling.

- The item is received later than expected.

- The order is canceled without notice because it is out of stock or no longer available, although not listed as such.

- The customer has difficulty returning an item and getting a refund.

- The buyer cannot reach the seller through e-mail, and no phone number is listed.

- The condition of the item is not as described.

- The model number or brand is different than the one ordered.

- The seller continually asks for positive feedback, and the customer does not like being hounded.

- The item was not discounted as expected.

Amazon sellers are constantly kept apprised of their customer performance numbers. To help sellers offer the highest quality experience for their buyers, Amazon developed the Performance Summary. With this summery, sellers can keep track of all sales, refunds, customer feedback, and the A-to-z Guarantee claims data. They are also able to readily see how their customer service is rated through the "View your performance summary" link on the Seller Account page. You can keep close track of your performance over the past month, or from month to month. In addition, you will be able to recall consolidated sales data and get information that will be helpful in determining your customers' levels of satisfaction. Those vendors that have success with their Amazon stores do whatever they can to achieve the highest feedback rating possible in regard to refund rates and A-to-z Guarantee claims. In most situations, the Amazon storeowners frequently offer their customers a highly satisfactory buying experience. Amazon will also give you tips if your feedback, refund rates, or A-to-z claims become too high.

This table defines the terms in the Performance Summary.

Term	Definition
SALES	
Total Value	The sum of ordered Gross Merchandise Sales (GMS) that successfully pass Marketplace Payments' fraud screen and credit-card process.
Orders	The number of orders that successfully pass Marketplace Payments' fraud screen and credit-card process.
Units Sold	The sum of ordered units that successfully pass Marketplace Payments' fraud screen and credit-card process.
REFUNDS	
Units Refunded	The number of units refunded based on post-order refund, cancellation, return, or goodwill adjustment.
Refund Rate	The percentage of units refunded based on units sold.
CUSTOMER FEEDBACK	
Total Ratings	The total number of feedback ratings received by the seller.
Negative Ratings	The total number of 1 or 2 feedback ratings received by the seller.
Negative Feedback Rate	The percentage of negative ratings based on total ratings.
GUARANTEE CLAIMS	
Total Value	The total value of A-to-z Guarantee claims granted in which the seller is accountable.
Claims Granted	The number of A-to-z Guarantee claims granted where the seller is accountable.

amazon.com

Amazon, Amazon.com and the Amazon.com logo are registered trademarks of Amazon.com, Inc. or its affiliates.

CHAPTER 21

Using E-mails to Foster Relationships

Because you do not actually see your clients, it is important to establish connections with them in other e-commerce ways. One of the most effective methods is e-mail. Electronic mail can be used to respond to questions about products, eliminate misunderstandings, prevent any problems arising in the future, and promote higher rankings in customer service all-around. The e-mails can also be used as a promotional tool for providing information on products and the theme of your Web site in general. As a vendor, you can use e-mails from customers to provide insights on trends and encourage you to make changes in your product listing when too many e-mails are making the same request.

When you receive an e-mail with a question about one of your products for sale, it is important to respond within 24 hours. You may want to consider having a separate e-mail just for queries, as they may get lost with all the other mail you get during the day. Take five minutes at the beginning of the day to check this account and respond to the customers. Even if you do not have the answer at that moment, or need additional information from the customer that is not noted in his or her e-mail, respond to the question. It is much better to send an e-mail with, "I'll check on that for you and will get back to you within 48 hours," or "Could you please give me more information regarding your concern?" than to respond late — or not at all. To speed up the process with responses to such queries, you can copy and paste in a general response. This is recommended over sending out form letters. Customers want to be treated like real people and communicate with real people — not automatons.

After a sale is made, e-mails are just as important. Amazon will e-mail you as soon as a sale is complete, along with the buyer's name and contact information. This information is also in your payments records. The customer is notified that the sale has been completed. At this point, you need to write your own e-mail to the customer, thanking them for placing the order, noting the specific item they purchased, and asking to be contacted in case of any problem with the order once received, or if there is a delay for any reason. You are building a rapport with the customer at the same time that you are taking a preventative stance.

You should also ask the customer to "opt in" to receive a newsletter that you publish every month or notice of sales events. (You will include a link where the customer can add his or her e-mail address and approve these monthly e-mails). There also may be an item that you have on sale at the present time that you can offer to the customer at a discount as a thank you for the present order. Give the customer a special code to use when buying the item. Lastly, put a post script (P.S.) on the e-mail reminding the buyer to "take a few minutes to leave feedback on Amazon about this transaction once receiving the item. A customer's input is always welcome."

Amazon reminds the buyer about a month after purchase to add feedback, if this has not already been done. This is another opportunity for you to contact the customer. You, once again, thank the customer for the order and confirm that everything received was as requested. As always, if there are any problems, you want to know. Then, stress the importance of buyer feedback in providing the best service possible and say, "If you have not had the opportunity to leave your personal feedback, it would be much appreciated at this time." Give the customer the link to the Amazon feedback page and, once again, offer your e-mail newsletter or tell them about another product of interest.

Making E-mail Friendly

- Write the e-mail in the same tone as if talking in person or on the phone with the customer. You can start off with a friendly "Hello, [first name of person]:" to set the tone and let the reader know that this is not an automated e-mail. You are a person talking to another person.

- Keep this friendly tone, no matter what the message. Even if the e-mail leaves you steaming, maintain your distance. Sometimes it is difficult to agree that "The customer is always right." You will only aggravate the situation if your response is discourteous. Also, always remember that everything you write is in print. This is not a telephone conversation; this is actual black-and-white evidence of your comments.

- Always reply to an e-mail, regardless if it is neutral, positive, negative, or a question, and respond as soon as possible. The person took the time to write the e-mail, so that means it is important. Your response does not have to be long — just enough to respond to the customer's comments. Set aside time first thing in the morning for responding to e-mails. Do not worry about any other aspect of your business at this time. Think of it as sending out advertisements to each of these individuals.

- If you do not have an answer to the customer's question, send an e-mail anyway. Give a time estimate on when you will e-mail again with the needed information. Make it as quick as possible.

- Do not use an automated response. You can copy and paste pertinent information or refer the person to "Help" links. Begin the e-mail with the personal greeting, and use your copy-and-paste response in the middle of the note where standard information is needed. This way, the customer is already feeling comfortable with the tone, and the standardized answer does not seem out of place. You have kept your time to a minimum, but made the customer feel good about writing. When someone takes the time to send an e-mail, a canned response is not well-received.

- Ask the customer to telephone if your answer is too difficult to respond to the question and several e-mails have gone back and forth without an understanding. Sometimes e-mail just does not work as well as discussing the issue over the phone. You do not want everyone calling, but certain situations become much easier and quicker with oral communication.

- Keep in mind different ways to handle difficult situations. Right from the beginning, acknowledge that you understand the customer's concern, and that you want to resolve any misunderstandings or problems. Most people do not ask for something beyond what was originally expected. It is just that the person's expectations are different than yours. There is no need to offer a free gift, which shows that you feel guilty, or go on and on about a small problem, such as a slight packaging error. Simply respond to the issue at hand and fulfill the expectation, if possible. If the customer did not understand the information correctly, offer a choice for a solution. Rather than refunding the entire amount, a compromise can be found if the communication is kept on a positive note.

- Write a follow-up e-mail if there was a problem and all has been resolved to the customer's satisfaction. Say that you were pleased to be of help and are available whenever any other need arises.

- At the end of all e-mails, always offer a "Thank you for your time and interest." You are starting on a friendly note and ending on one. Keep a file of these responses, just in case something arises in the future with a particular customer, or in order to see trends.

 **CHAPTER 22**

Get Noticed with Search Engine Optimization

With millions of online stores, how do you get customers to your Web site? Amazon gives you a boost on being found by the masses. Yet this is not enough. You need to ensure that customers get to your site by doing your own online marketing and getting a high rank in the search engines. Search engine optimization, or SEO, has long been one of the hottest topics in online marketing. Everyone has his or her own suggestions on how to best get a high ranking on the search engines. When someone who is not that familiar with the Internet listens to these online "gurus" talk about SEO, it sounds as if they are discussing something about another dimension. A whole book could be written about this topic, and actually many have. But it is not all that complicated of a concept.

Basically, it comes down to imagining a huge spider stretching its eight legs out across the world to all the millions of Web sites looking for prey — in this case, words and phrases. Its legs are more apt to grasp some phrases more than others. These spiders, or search engines, gather, retrieve, and organize information to have the most relevant results, based on the keywords requested by users.

Search engine spiders therefore decipher the context of your Web pages and rank your content by looking for specific phrases. They use two or more related words or phrases to glean the basic meaning of your page. In all your online communication, it is necessary for you to provide that relevant copy with the words and phrases that will most attract these spiders. On a bicycle blog, if you use the phrase "bicycle safety" a reasonable number of times, the search engines know that your page is generally about bicycles and, more specifically, bicycle safety. If the word is also placed in the title, then the search engines recognize that the article, and perhaps the whole site, is about that item. If it gets enough information from your pages that the site is about bicycles, it will rank the site for not only bicycles, but also similar terms.

Bottom line: There are key phrases — studies show that longer words grouped together do better than shorter ones — to use on your blog to attract the search engines and thus those who search with them. You can also find out what phrases are searched most and how popular certain search terms are across geographic regions, cities, and languages. There are some basics that you can do to increase the chances that the search engines will pick up your copy. You should:

- Put at least a couple of new posts on your Web site or blog every week that are not picked up from someplace else word-for-word. The search engines like new material. This also gives you an opportunity to write about any other information regarding your products.

- Remember to link your Web site to your blog and vice versa. On your Web site, you should have a teaser about the latest information and a link to the blog. Offer something as a giveaway, or have a contest to encourage visitors to click on the link.

- Have links on your blog that go back to your Web site, but not an overwhelming number. They should be incorporated into the copy and not just standing alone. Search engines look at the copy around links to see if they match related copy.

- Start several different blogs for various niches of audiences you want to reach, if you have the time. Build your Web site with a number of different pages. This gives you additional opportunities with the search engines. Every page you have online gives you another means for using key words that will be searched and reach specific potential customers. You can end up with hundreds of content pages, each one that can be indexed by the search engines. In your copy, use the key words that visitors search for the most.

- Keep quality in mind at all times. You want strong editorial content that will be of interest to your readers and the search engines.

CASE STUDY: DAVE TAYLOR

Dave Taylor

www.askdavetaylor.com

Dave Taylor hooked up with the Internet right from its beginning in 1980 and is widely recognized as an expert on both technical and business issues. He has published materials on numerous related topics, launched four Internet-related startup companies, written 20 business and technical books, and holds both a master's in business administration and in education. Taylor maintains three Weblogs: "The Business Blog" at **www.intuitive.com**, focused on business and industry analysis; the eponymous "Ask Dave Taylor," devoted to technical and business issues; and "The Attachment Parenting Blog," at **www.apparenting.com**, discussing topics of parental interest. He is an award-winning speaker and frequent guest on radio and podcast programs, and with conferences and workshops. He is also an Amazon Associate and offers advice for other Associate members. Here, Taylor provides an easy-to-understand overview on search engine optimization.

- When it comes to search engine optimization, I think about "findability," or how easy is it for potential customers to locate you when searching online for a product or service. Two major aspects of findability are most important to consider. The first involves your Web site design and structure, and the second deals with developing into a recognized and credible site.

- When designing and writing copy for your Web site, you need to identify keywords or phrases that your potential customers will be using in their online search. If you are a toy store, your keywords might be "toy store" or "toy store Chicago," but they might also be for specialties, like "Fisher Price Illinois" or "discount toys." The more specific your keywords, the better results you can obtain. It goes without saying that it is much easier to rank well in the search engine ratings for "green cleaning supplies Waukegan, Illinois" than "cleaning supplies."

- Once you make that list — and you need to come up with at least 100 keywords — conduct "keyword research" to determine which

CASE STUDY: DAVE TAYLOR

of these are the most used in a search. For example, I like to use **www.wordtracker.com**. It is worth the time and effort. It is not of value using phrases in your Web copy if there is only one person who inputs those words each month. Now you can snake those words and phrases into your Web copy, page titles, article headlines, and blog entries. A toy store site has a specific page about "discount name-brand toys" that may cover the advantages and disadvantages of some of these toys and include a "buy from us" button to turn readers into customers.

- According to Google's "Webmaster Guidelines," it is necessary for you to provide descriptive text for page titles and headlines and even filenames to help the search engines properly categorize your information. That's why "Welcome to Ace Toy Store" is not effective, while "Ace Toy Store: Your first stop for discount name-brand toys" is better and "Discount Name-Brand Toys from Ace Toy Store of Chicago" is better. Also keep in mind that each and every page on your Web site must have a different descriptive title.

- The other important element of search engine optimization is "inbound links." One of the most important aspects of SEO is deciding which of the millions of pages that match a given query will be most popular. Time and time again, the results are the same: If you have good content, lots of people will link to your site. Therefore, better content means better SEO results, which means more people to buy your product.

Watch Out for Search Engine "No-Nos"

Sometimes, Web site SEO pros go overboard when trying to get recognition for their Web site through the search engines; they resort to unacceptable routines like keyword stuffing. This does not work: The copy is uninteresting, and the search engines do not like the tricks. The recommended keyword density ranges from 3 to 7 percent, and anything above this, even 10 percent density, begins to look a great deal like keyword stuffing and most likely will be ignored by the search engines. It is even more important to have the correct density in the title, the headings, and the first paragraphs. Use a word-density tool to determine if your key-words are in the correct range. If not, find synonyms or rewrite the copy. At the same time, make sure that you do not have too many words in italic or bold face; these will also not attract the search engines if not in the correct quantity.

Hidden texts are another non-acceptable way of getting maximum optimization with search engines. This is when the text and links are made the same color as the background. Search engines will not just ignore these, but may penalize Web sites for such practices. Very similar to hidden links are doorway pages, which are written for high ranking in the search engines and not for human reading. Duplicate pages, with the same copy used over and over again, are similarly nixed. These are also no longer acceptable. The search engines are just as stringent on the number of links per page both outbound and inbound links. There are also programs that can let you know if your link density is acceptable.

Another SEO turn-off is using small or unreadable type to fit more words into the design of the Web Site. The biggest "do not" in terms of keywords is one that not only disturbs the search engines, but the visitors as well. Do not put keywords into your copy that have nothing to do with the theme of the page. Today, keywords are nonetheless important, but it is how they are used that matters.

CHAPTER 23

Making a Stand-Out, Outstanding Web Site

A Web site that only has products listed or shown will not entice visitors to stay or to come back often. In addition, it will not rank high with the search engines that are looking for good content. Although it is suggested to set up a blog (see below), you still want your Web site to be informative and interesting. You may conduct an aggressive advertising campaign, implement a multifaceted viral marketing program, and participate in several affiliate programs, but if your Web site is not content-rich, you are not going to bring in traffic. Content that is helpful, entertaining, valuable, informative, and educational can attract and retain visitors and potential customers more than any other promotional tool.

If your Web site has only products and prices, do not expect a lot of return traffic. But regularly updating your site's content can enhance credibility and make you more competitive. People will want to return to your site because they know they can always learn something new about their personal interest. It is essential that your Web site immediately lets your visitors know they came to the right place for what they want. If you can meet your visitors' needs, then display this information clearly and concisely on all your Web site pages.

The Web site is important to 1) to show off and sell your merchandise, 2) to build community and traffic, and 3) to increase the search engine optimization ranking. Placing SEO keywords into the copy needs to be done on all your Web pages. You also need to clearly define your company and its products on each page, as visitors can come in on any page on your site. How often does a search engine send you to a page that has interesting information, but you do not know where it originated? The Internet is not like reading a book with a beginning and end. On a Web site, visitors can go in various different directions. Unless you redirect them to your homepage, they may never get there to buy your products.

At the very least, have a similar header and footer on each page, with a menu and links of additional pages. You should also have a brief paragraph at the top left corner of each page to orient the reader. What Web site is associated with this page? What information can you find here? How does the visitor get back home? This not only helps the searcher know what to expect, but it provides additional information for the search engines.

Web site writing does not have to be like writing a best-selling novel. It just needs to be descriptive and have creative use of the keywords that people may enter into the search engines for this information. You want to let the users know about the products and information they can find in the pages of your Web site, and the search engines know what people can find when they arrive. Adding keyword phrases does not mean that it is proper to write a sentence such as, "Drinking dairy milkshakes is like drinking dairy milkshakes." It is easy to pick out Web sites that have been inaccurately optimized because the same word is used in headlines, copy, and links even when they do not make sense. Nor is it appropriate to write hard sales copy that promises that you can offer everything under the sun. People see enough advertisements during the day; they are going to your Web site to learn something, not be bombarded with hard sell.

The following are different ideas for adding to your homepage and additional pages. Of course, you do not want to include all these on your homepage. Yet in follow-up pages, you are able to offer the readers a great deal more solid material. If you have a blog, remember to include an update notice to let visitors know there is new information. Include a table of contents on your homepage with the information available on other pages and a site map. People look for information in different ways.

Voice Your Own Thoughts

You want to use your expertise to rate products and recommend which ones are best depending on the situation. This does not only have to be products that you are selling; it can be books, music, clothing, restaurants, artwork, or anything of interest to others. If they respect your input about the products you sell, they want to hear about your other thoughts as well. But nor do you always have to agree with everyone else. There is nothing like good controversy to raise interest. If you feel differently from others about a book you have read or a movie that everyone is discussing, do not be afraid to shake things up a little.

This will also encourage other people to write in, which is another way to get visitors to keep coming back to you site. As an expert, you can also evaluate other Web sites and Internet resources, such as e-books and e-zine articles. This interaction with your visitors establishes closer relationships, helps you better understand their needs and interests, gives them a means for addressing their suggestions and complaints, provides an avenue for their feedback on your products and services, and assists in building a loyal community. At the same time, you are getting fresh content for your site that both the visitors and search engines love.

What Do Your Visitors Think?

Another way of inviting people to your Web site is by taking a poll or survey on a specific product or topic of interest that has to do with your theme. For example, if you sell DVDs and CDs, you can ask your visitors about their feelings on the latest trend of product placement, where advertisements are subtly integrated with online quasi-documentaries and real-life situations. Or you can ask, "What did you think of this week's editorial?" A survey is no longer than eight questions, with "yes" and "no" responses. This can give you more information about your visitors' demographics. Offer a discount or free e-book to those people who participate. This is also another way to generate names for e-zines and e-mails. Just make sure that people agree or "opt in" to this service.

You can also ask your customers for comments on your business and Web site. What do they like or do not like? What would they change? What suggestions do they have for other information? How was their buying experience? Be sure to provide an overview of results, if you decide to take this route. Your readers will want to know what others thought.

Encourage a Give-and-Take Relationship

You always want to hear from your customers and other visitors. The more that they participate and become involved with your Web site, the more they will be willing to turn to you when buying your specific product line. Getting feedback also gives you a better indication on whether your products are on-par with the demographics or need to be altered. For example, if you are getting mostly baby boomers to your Web site, you may want to add products that are more geared to older consumers, or better highlight those that you already sell.

Your visitors also like to hear from one another, as they become part of a community of people who have similar interests. On every page, offer a link for an e-mail address or feedback form to let visitors write in with their comments, opinions, and suggestions. You should also noticeably display the company's full name, phone and fax number, and physical location. Some e-commerce sites only include an e-mail or, even less frequently, an e-mail form. As online consumers have become savvier, they are starting to shy away from those Web sites that do not provide specific contact information.

"All About Us" Information

Similarly, people want to know about your business. How do they know you are reputable, offer a reliable service, and provide quality product for their money if they do not know anything about you? Being associated with Amazon is a big plus for credibility. But more references are needed. People want input. Who are you? What products do you sell? How many years have you been in business? Why should they purchase an item from you instead of the hundreds of other vendors who sell similar merchandise? What are your quality standards? What features and benefits do you offer? How do you rate with your customers? Prospective customers who are making a buying decision should be able to find all the facts they need to make that choice without having to call or e-mail you for more information.

The No. 1 Source

Your visitors are curious and want to increase their knowledge base. Offer a library of articles that may be of interest, in addition to your own blog and newsletter articles. If you are keeping up with changes in your products or your industry in general, you probably read a number of items of interest. Do not provide a link to those articles, because you do not want to lose your potential customers as they wander off to another site. Rather, copy them right into your library and give credit to the source. If the article is copyrighted, it might be a good idea to clear this with the owner of the information to avoid copyright infringement. Always let the sources know that you are adding their information to your Web site. Reciprocity is a great way to let people on other sites know about your products.

Get a FAQs Page

A Frequently Asked Questions (FAQs) page can provide information to your visitors, build trust, and keep you from getting the same questions over and over again. Even if you do get an e-mail on the subject, you can respond by giving the link for additional information. The FAQs should, at minimum, help visitors learn more about products that are listed, explain how to order products, provide information on shipping and days to receipt, give an overview of the refund policy, tell how to give feedback for a product and service, and how to reach the company.

Depending on your Web site and other communications and offerings, such as blogs, e-zines, e-mails, and special bonus days, your FAQ will have different questions and answers. When you write it, put on your "customer hat," so you can cover as much needed information as possible.

Testimonials and Positive Comments

From time to time, you will receive an e-mail from a customer who is pleased with your service and/or products. E-mail back with a thank you and ask if the comments can be made public with or without a name. Whenever other media, such as a Web site or newspaper, mentions your company, be sure to highlight that on the homepage.

Clean Web Site Design

Web site visitors like pages that are clean, clear, and easy to read and navigate. It is fine to use widgets or other design elements to spark up your page, but too many bells and whistles make the readers too disinterested to stay put. Grammatical and spelling errors on Web sites reflect the quality of your products. Poor Web design does the same. When the Web first started, everyone's page looked the same, with straight copy and a variety of colors. Then, when new design elements came in, such as animated gifs, audio, and video, there were numerous pages that were weighed down with way too many extras.

Now, as ever, the best approach is moderation. Because visitors like pages that download quickly and with easy-to-find, relevant copy, find a good compromise between too much and too little copy and design. Just as in print, white space is important in Web design as well. You do not want to cram too much onto a page or have such small type that it is barely readable. You also want the visitors to find the Table of Contents easily. Yet, you do not want links on the top, sides and bottom of each page. Having this information in multiple places will be helpful. Just because you see a design that works well at one Web site does not mean that it will be just as effective for yours. Similar to your Web site copy, you need to know what is best for your visitors. You can also run surveys about your design, similar to those mentioned for Web site copy, to see if you are meeting your users' visual needs and interests.

Privacy and Safety/Security Assurance

Amazon is gathering information about your customers at all times. It is important for your visitors to know your affiliation with Amazon and the company's privacy notice. Supply a link for more information. Customers should also be given the link to Amazon's safety and security tips, and to the A-to-z Guarantee plan.

Your Amazon.com Bill of Rights

1. Safe shopping. When you shop Amazon, you'll be one of millions of customers who have safely shopped with us without credit card fraud. If you feel more comfortable, you may enter only your card's last five digits and its expiration date for most online purchases. Once you have fully submitted your order, you may phone in the rest of your card number.

2. No obligation. Our Personal Notification Services, such as Amazon.com Alerts and E-mail Me When Available, are provided free of charge, and you are under no obligation to buy anything.

3. Unsubscribing. You can unsubscribe or change your subscription to any of our Personal Notification Services at any time. Simply visit your Amazon.com Subscriptions page to modify your subscriptions online.

4. Amazon.com Updates. As a customer, subscriber, or contest entrant, you will occasionally receive e-mail updates about important functionality changes to the Web site, new Amazon.com services, and special offers we think you'll find valuable. But if you'd rather not receive them, please visit your Amazon.com Subscriptions page to change your preferences.

5. Privacy. Amazon.com knows that you care about how information about you is used and shared, and we appreciate the trust that you place in us. That's why we post a Privacy Notice in our store. Simply stated, our Privacy Notice explains what information we collect from you, how we use that information, and what choices you have with respect to that information.

amazon.com·

Amazon, Amazon.com and the Amazon.com logo are registered
trademarks of Amazon.com, Inc. or its affiliates.

CHAPTER 24

Building Ties with the Online Community

Community is a word that quite clearly describes the Internet. Although people are from all over the world and from completely different walks of life, they find similar interests online and come together to share their thoughts and listen and learn, support and oppose others. To be successful with an Amazon site, you need to establish yourself as a part of this community and as an expert in a particular area that is in line with the product you sell. There are a variety of ways of doing this.

Establishing Credibility with a Blog

Besides taking advantage of the support that Amazon gives you through its widgets and banners, community building, and sales items, one of the best ways to build online popularity and increase your ratings with the search engines is through blogs. Short for Web logs, blogs are a combination of online newsletter, forum, and journal that revolve around a specific theme related to your Amazon Associates Web site, WebStore, or any other Web site or business you have established to sell your Amazon products. You may, for example, build a Web site in conjunction with the book or CD you have listed with Amazon Advantage. Your blog can include links to your Amazon Web site and/or sell the actual product.

The main purpose of the blog is to provide relevant and up-to-date information on your established theme. If you sell racing bicycles, for example, your blog can have postings on newly introduced bicycles, safety recommendations, product alerts, bicycle comparisons, or just your own thoughts on certain cycling issues. Remember, in the minds of your potential buyer, information is one of your most essential products. Offering relevant and up-to-date information:

- Builds community.

- Makes you a credible source for visitors.

- Keeps people returning to your blog for more information and education.

- Encourages visitors to follow your lead with suggested products to buy, and to go to your Web site and purchase them.

- Helps you build customer lists, which is a must with online marketing.

- Gives your visitors an opportunity to become involved with your blog with feedback.

- Offers a means of education about your products or services.

- Helps you monitor the interests and feedback of the users.

- Offers relevant material for the search engines.

- Enhances your listing rank with the search engines.

- Allows you the opportunity to introduce new products.

- Sells more of your products.

Starting a blog is easier than ever because of the friendly blog platforms available to produce them. It is the upkeep that is much more time-consuming. Once starting a blog, it is necessary to keep on feeding it with articles. The most effective way to start small is to create a free blog with one of the many platforms easily available. Some of the most widely used platforms to build a blog are WordPress, Blogger®, and LiveJournal®.

Regardless of which blog platform you decide to choose when creating your blog, you will be led step-by-step with some type of tutorial. When you read the instructions on the respective blog platform, you will find all necessary information. Creating a blog can take as little as 15 minutes. There will be different templates from which to choose. The blog setup is usually straightforward and does not require any coding knowledge. This is only necessary once you want to start to personalize your blog and get into more complex design. For your purposes, this will most likely not be necessary. You also have your Web site, which has more of the bells and whistles.

WordPress is an especially robust blogging software for start-up. You can create a WordPress blog for free in minutes, and just as quickly write a post. Before you start your blog, you should also spend a few hours traveling online and looking at some of the competitors' blogs for ideas for layout and design, articles, and promotional tools. Also start looking for some blogs that will be appropriate for sharing links. This will begin to expand your audience readership.

From the start, you should always remember consistency and patience. Studies report that there are millions of blogs online, but a large number of these were started and never continued. Another large group never attracted the search engines and are sitting in some online limbo land. Unless you can 1) generate a blog post at least two times a week and 2) continue to do so until you begin to get higher listings on search engines and visitors to the blog, nothing will happen. This can take several months. Too many people do not build up their blog vehicle because they do not write enough posts or have the patience to wait for responses.

You need a topic that is going to be of interest to your intended visitors and that is related to your product line or theme for your book or Web site. This will also take some research. You have to think carefully about the people you want to target and their interests. Then you need a subject that you know well, is wide enough to write about on a regular basis, and that is constantly changing and offering something of interest for your readers. Because your blog is about your business, you can write about product industry news you read about in the newspapers, business publications, or online.

Remember that you need to have a link back to your Web site in the article, so your blog post has to relate somehow to the products you are selling. No one is looking for a scholarly, in-depth report on a subject; just a few personal comments can be enough. If you hit a block on ideas for your postings, respond to someone else's blog on a similar topic. Include a link to this other blog in your blog post and then send the author of that blog an e-mail about the link. This not only provides a topic on which to write, but goodwill with another blogger who already has ratings established. It is very possible that this blogger will respond by sending a link back to you.

Encourage responses from your own readers. This, too, builds community and lends credibility to both your blog and Web site. Also, it may give you additional blog and Web sites with which to link. When someone does respond, include a "thank you" on the blog page or send the person an e-mail. Once your blog begins to get a following, list it with the blog directories. That will encourage more people to visit and respond, and also enable additional search engine listings. There are thousands of blog directories available for submitting your blogs, and many more directories created daily.

Again, patience is the key. You will not be able to register with most of the directories immediately. You have to build up your blog first, as the directories will want a certain number of posts written in your blog before you can be listed. Also, some of the directories are free, and others will charge for their services. Some directories generate very little traffic, with a lot of categories and few listings under them, and low ranking in the search engines. In other words, especially if you are paying to be listed in a directory, you need to make sure that you are getting your money's worth. After you sign up with a directory, keep track of the traffic that is or is not being generated, and determine if the directory is of value.

Here is the list of some of the major blog directories:

1. **Best of the Web Blog Directory** is one of the earliest directories. It is very selective and accepts blogs that are in existence for six months or more of postings.

2. **Eaton Web Blog Directory** claims to be the oldest such publication. Once listed in this directory, look for an automatic increase in visitors. Each accepted blog is ranked on strength, momentum, and overall content.

3. **Blog Directory//Blog Catalog** is another older listing that has a wide range of categories and allows various searching modes.

4. **Blog Flux** is a directory with a wide variety of categories in alphabetical order. It also offers many useful tools for bloggers.

5. **Blogarama** has more than 80,000 blogs listed with both free and paid listings.

6. **Blogoogle** also has free and paid blog submission. Blogs listed for free must have a specific page rank. They are very strict on who they do and do not accept, so carefully read the Web site.

7. **Bloggeries** has strong categories and subcategories with a clear and concise layout where readers are able to find their blogs very quickly and efficiently.

8. **Bloggapedia's** homepage attracts readers who are interested in top blogs and new posts. There are also different categories from the norm.

The Benefits of Blogs

- Search engines, like blogs, usually have new and up-to-date information, and blogs are designed to reach out to the search engines.

- The more valuable, solid information you have, the greater the chances for attracting traffic.

- Visitors normally would rather read content on a subject that interests them than go to a business product page.

- Content in blogs is picked up by other bloggers and gives you more exposure and traffic.

- People who like the copy on a blog because it is fresh and informative will return again and again.

- Blogs can create a brand just as easily, if not more easily, than other vehicles. Through the copy content and style, you create an image about yourself and your business.

- You establish relationships with your visitors, who spread the word to others who have similar interests.

- Visitors are looking for credible experts who can answer their questions and help them reach their goals, and your blog can fulfill this need.

- When the time comes to purchase a product, your blog visitors will know where to turn.

Building a Customer List

A blog serves another purpose: Growing your customer community. On your blog and Web site, you need to give your visitors an opportunity to sign up for additional information. In order to refrain from any problems with spam, you must 1) let people know exactly what they will receive by "opting in," or agreeing to have their name added to a list. Are they signing up for e-mail notification for sales, monthly e-zines with information about a specific topic related to your product line, weekly e-mail updates, a video, a free e-book? Give them only what they have agreed to receive; 2) promise, and keep the promise, that you will not give or sell their names to any other vendor or service. In a brick-and-mortar business, organizations use advertising, promotions, free giveaways, and contests to develop a list that is used for future marketing purposes. Online, it is difficult to build this list because there are millions of enterprises and millions of people out in the virtual world. Customer list-building is one of the first things to figure out if you are going to build your online business, as the targeted list will be the lifeblood of your revenue streams.

Many of the reports you receive from Amazon will also have specific information about customers. This is vital data to build your business. It will also help you break down your lists into specific categories, be they by geography, product, or customer demographic.

On your Web site and blog, you want to give visitors the means to opt in for more information, or for some type of giveaway or contest. Another way of building a list is to write and place articles on the Web with internal links, signature, or biographical information to your blog or Web site. You are building your name recognition and credibility at the same time that you are acquiring names and e-mail addresses. Contributing a weekly article to a number of different specialized article directories offers you an effective way to drive traffic to your product or service. In most article directories, you are allowed to give yourself as the author and add a signature. Usually, you can put a one-line descriptor with your signature and/or your Web site address. For example, "Bikeshop.com, where all your biking needs are cycled quickly."

Another marketing approach is opt-in e-mail, or sending specialized business electronic mail to recipients who have already approved the receipt of commercial messages. This can be accomplished through services, or "safe lists," where you agree to receive e-mails from other business owners/service providers in exchange for having your own e-mail sent to targeted recipients. The usual opt-in e-mail service permits one post per week.

Similarly, co-registration is when someone refers leads, subscriptions, or memberships with a partner. That is, you and someone with a similar product exchange links and sign-ups on each other's sites. Online, you can find a list of co-registration services offering leads on a fee basis. Just as with the blog directories, you need to review the sites and determine which may be best for you and, after signing up, keep track of results. You can combine your goal of providing information along with building a list. You can offer a weekly e-zine or newsletter, a series of informative e-mails, or an e-book. These offer valuable information, subtly promote your products, and build up a customer list.

Your e-book can also be used for many other promotional vehicles. Once you have generated this list, you can use it to keep your name in the forefront of the customer's mind. On a quarterly basis, you can send out specific product news and/or coupons. Repetition — but not spamming — works to sell products or services in the long run, assuming that the individual has given you permission.

On your blog, you can also have a discussion area. Your readers and potential customers can become their own community by being able to write in different topics of interest. There are always provocative or controversial subjects in addition to informational ones.

Joining Forums

You can also spread your expertise to other online locations, such as other blogs, message boards, and forums. The important thing to keep in mind is subtlety. You do not want to join theme-related forums just to promote your products. In fact, this is the easiest way for you to get thrown out. You can do a search for forums or message boards through Google or any other search engine. For example, if you are selling bicycles, put the words "bicycle forum" into the search engine. Here are some of the different forums that come up: road cycling, single-speed and fixed gar, commuting, bicycle mechanics, 50+, folding bikes, touring, and mountain biking.

Once you have seen a few forums that appear promising, look at each one and see how many people have been sending messages, the quality of these messages (some forums are just another means for advertising and marketing), and how often people write in. You want a large, active community that is looking for information. Find three of these forums and then just read them for a week or so. Get a feel for the forum first in regard to its style and needs. For example, some are very social, but others want more technical information.

When you feel that you understand the culture, respond to the some of the comments by offering advice. Do not push your products or services. The more you offer information, the more known you will become, and the more people will come to your site. Your comments may also be picked up by the search engines, depending on the format. When you register, you will be able to include the same, or similar, signature to the one you have at the end of your e-zine articles. You can tailor your signature for the subject of the forum and the people you are targeting. You can also respond to comments made on other blogs. These are seen by all the readers of that blog, an entirely different group of people, and may also be picked up by the search engines.

Product Reviews

As noted, people are always looking for additional information and expertise. As an Amazon representative, you offer this knowledge. You can provide your experience by reviewing products. For instance, what if you have had an experience with barbeque smokers? Because you have that knowledge, you can write reviews on other products in the same area. Next to every product on Amazon is a link for a product review. Your comments do not have to be in-depth, just clear and to the point. Each review gives you two links — one for your name and one for the product you have reviewed.

You can also write a review on a book about summer backyard cooking or building a backyard kitchen. If readers enjoy your review or find it valuable, they will see what else you have written on your blog and also inquire more about the products you sell online. Once again, be subtle. You should not say, "This is a great product and you can find more like it on my Web site." Your comments must be truthful and sincere. It is better, for example, for you to talk about your own vendors: "Over the years, I've carried a number of different brands of smokers, and I get the best feedback about (x brand). This new product has a lot of bells and whistles, but customers keep on coming back for the tried-and-true models."

Video Reviews

amazon.com

Amazon, Amazon.com and the Amazon.com logo are registered trademarks of Amazon.com, Inc. or its affiliates.

Amazon now allows customers to upload product video reviews. Use a Webcam or video camera to record and upload reviews. Amazon values its reviews so much, in fact, that customers can choose who they consider "Top Reviewers." In this case, it is not quantity for reviews, but quality. After a customer reads a review, he or she can push a "yes" or "no" button on whether or not the information was helpful, based on accuracy and expertise. If you become a "Top Reviewer," you will be given a special badge of accommodation.

Earlier "Listmania" was mentioned in regard to the Advantage program. Another way to get free publicity on Amazon is by using this "Listmania" function. As an expert, you can make a list of items that have especially influenced you. You can include books on your list, in addition to music, DVDs and videos, electronics, toys and games, software, computers and video games, kitchen tools and hardware, and lawn and patio furniture. As with the reviews, customers can rate this list and also e-mail it to others, if they found it helpful. Add this list to your Amazon profile by just clicking on the "Add a Listmania" link on the left side of the "Friends and Favorites" homepage.

The "So you would like to…" listing on Amazon is yet another way for you to promote your knowledge. This takes more writing skill than making a list, but it also adds weight to your credibility and visibility. Make sure that you let the readers know what gives you the right to be the expert in this field; let them know how long you have been using or selling similar products. "This product is great," says nothing. "This product is great because…," or "I find when barbecuing on this smoker, it is best to leave the roast in at least 10 hours," lends credibility. You can write about any product with an Amazon Standard Identification Number (ASIN) or ISBN number and create your entry by clicking on "So you would like to…" guide on the left side of the "Friends and Favorites" homepage.

Amazon also gives buyers an opportunity to leave feedback on their merchants and rate them on their performance. A summary of this feedback from your buyers — including an average of your 1-to-5-star rating — accompanies your name whenever you list an item at Amazon. Sellers are rewarded and receive positive feedback for communicating well and shipping quickly. If you receive a negative rating, accept it as constructive criticism. It is best for you to take the suggestions in a good light and thank the customers for their input.

CHAPTER 25

Conclusion: Continuous Change at Amazon

There is always something new being introduced at Amazon. The IT people are continuously working in the background to stay ahead of the latest technology. If you look on the Web Services solutions page, there are always betas being tested.

Shoppers can use their cell phone to reach an Amazon store and text message for a comparison of any item name, UPC code, or ISBN number. If the price is right, the customer can order it from Amazon via replying to the text message. It also sends a link to the product page, so the user can browse more details. The response comes back within seconds. This is a great way for your customers to see if they can save a few dollars by buying a product online from you versus at a brick-and-mortar business.

New widgets are regularly being added. For retailers, there is the Amazon Flexible Payment Service (FPS) marketplace widget that offers Web site developers the ability to transfer money between two other parties, with complete control of fees paid to the developer. The new widget helps developers create shopping carts, e-commerce platforms, and marketplaces. E-commerce service providers, shopping cart providers, or marketplace application developers can use this widget to facilitate payments between buyers and sellers.

The "Pay Now" widget, a quick way to accept payments on your Web site, is enhanced. These widgets, with their easy-to-use HTML function, allow you to copy and paste in the FPS. This can be the only payment or one of the alternative payment methods on your site. The "static button" can easily get you started. You use this button to create a Web page that requests payment when you already know the amount customers are going to be charged for an item. After a payment is processed, Amazon returns the reference ID, an Amazon payments transaction ID, and the payment status to your Web site. Also, all the information related to your transactions is available at your payments account. After processing a transaction, Amazon payments sends notification e-mails to you and your customers.

Amazon, Amazon.com and the Amazon.com logo are registered trademarks of Amazon.com, Inc. or its affiliates.

You can upgrade your static button to the "dynamic button" at any time, if necessary. This dynamic widget can be used when you may want to alter the price on a regular basis. For instance, you sell a number of different items, and the customer is charged based on the product(s) selected or you charge different shipping rates based on the customer's choice. Use the dynamic button when selling a number of different products and not wanting to use the widget creation form to make a button for each product. You can create a button once and customize it each time you display it on your site.

The "alternative payment method" widget is used when you want to offer Amazon payments as a choice in addition to an existing payment option on your site. For instance, you want to offer Amazon payments as well as your credit card offering or other payment method. Third-party developers such as e-commerce solution and shopping cart providers and marketplace application developers can use this widget to facilitate payments between buyers and sellers. You can also use the widget to charge a marketplace fee to your sellers for using your Web site/application.

The "video" widget gives Associates commissions from Amazon product links embedded in the videos. You can create new videos to promote specific products or use ones you already have produced and incorporate them into the Amazon widget tool. After watching your video, people will have the option of adding your video to their own site. Associates have an option of showing straight product information, something new about the theme of the Web site, or anything that is just plain nonsensical or serious. With this widget, Associates can earn money when viewers follow the links and purchase products. They can also easily add pop-ups to existing videos and have price and product information appear anywhere in the video.

The service health dashboard, on Amazon's back end, provides access to current status and historical data about Amazon Web Services offerings. This gives developers and users a means to determine how well the Amazon platform is operating. If there is a problem with a service, you can expand the appropriate line in the details section.

The Mechanical Turk enables developers at different companies to programmatically access an on-demand workforce. They are able to rely on the feature to build human intelligence right into different applications. Computing technology may be always improving, but many things still can be done better by humans rather than computers, such as identification of objects in a photograph or video, carrying out data duplication, transcription of audio recordings, and conducting research on data specifics. Over the years, companies have hired temporary workforces to finish these types of tasks. The goal of the Mechanical Turk is to easily and cost-effectively access human intelligence.

The name Mechanical Turk stems back a couple of hundred years. In 1769, Hungarian nobleman Wolfgang von Kempelen amazed Europe by constructing a mechanical chess-playing automaton that beat almost every player. In the display, a life-sized wooden mannequin, adorned in fur-garnished clothing and turban, sat on a wooden cabinet to represent the automaton. The device toured Europe and bested such intelligent competitors as Benjamin Franklin and Napoleon Bonaparte. To respond to people who were skeptical, Kempelen revealed complicated workings that powered his mechanized chess player. He made everyone believe that he had developed a machine that could apply artificial intelligence. No one knew that a chess master was cleverly concealed inside.

Companies are using the Amazon Mechanical Turk service, which consists of the brain power of actual people around the world, for a variety of services. For instance, this service lets companies ensure the high quality of its work. When many people offer the same answer, a function can be approved. Other organizations rely on the Mechanical Turk to find duplicate entries in directories or catalogues and verify item details, such as phone numbers and hours of operation. They are also relying on this service to gather a wide variety and extent of information that would not be possible otherwise, such as letting individuals ask questions from a computer or mobile device about a specific topic and allowing people to respond with their results, complete survey data on numerous subjects, complete reviews, descriptions, and blog entries for Web sites, and find specific fields of data elements in huge private and public documents. Some companies are leveraging the power of the Mechanical Turk to complete podcast editing and transcription, translations and rate the accuracy of search engine results.

With the Mechanical Turk, companies define "HITs," or the specific information that they are seeking at the lowest price. The clearer the guidance given the user to accomplish the HIT, the better the outcome, and the more people will complete the work at a faster pace. The best HITs explain specifically how a query should be answered and what needs to be done for the accurate response. In most cases, workers are qualified before being permitted to complete tasks. These can consist of finishing a brief series of questions or simple duties that must be done. In some cases, workers need to answer a minimum number of their submitted HITs correctly before taking on additional assignments. Qualifying workers allows companies to choose a particular demographic of workers and/or to train the workforce in what type of response is required. Payment for the HITs is handled through Amazon Payments.

Although the work is quite mechanical and pays only cents to a few dollars, thousands of people from the United States and other countries worldwide have completed tasks on **www.mturk.com.** Some of the tasks include tagging a variety of images with labels to help with searches in a database and pairing a company with its industry, such as information technology, human resources, or health care. This does not command much mind power, nor take long, but people find it fun and interesting and a good way of learning more about how the online system works. Companies get thousands of workers at a low cost doing the work in a short period of time.

The Online World to Come

Despite the ups and downs of the marketplace, a number of trends bode well for those who now get on the online e-commerce bandwagon. An Art Technology Group survey found that many of the most well-known Web stores plan on maintaining or growing e-commerce investments in the coming years. Changes in consumer spending do not greatly influence their e-commerce business, or may even have a beneficial impact resulting in this expansion. The survey acquired information from 50 global brands in industries including a broad spectrum of retail, media and entertainment, financial services and insurance, telecommunications, consumer product manufacturing, health care, and technology consulting. Although all respondents had a minimum of $10 million in Web sales, most, or 58 percent of participants, reported annual Web sales of at least $100 million, and 26 percent of these said annual Web sales were at least $1 billion.

Specifically, the research showed that:

- 96 percent of respondents plan on either maintaining or increasing their level of investment in e-commerce or ways to improve the customers' Web buying experiences.

- Of all those who responded, 4 percent reported they would invest less in e-commerce so they could focus on other marketing and sales channels.

- It is reported that 48 percent of those surveyed state that any slowing of U.S. economy would not significantly impact e-commerce business.

- 22 percent of respondents believed the slowing U.S. economy may lead to a positive impact on Web business, which results in e-commerce expansion.

- Sellers report tools as improved search strategies as essential for gaining digital dollars with an emphasis on building loyalty, as consumers have fewer dollars in general to spend. The overall conclusion was that consumers are looking for bargains and ways to save gas and thus are turning to the Web. "...so the time is now

> to take advantage of the opportunity to delight new customers and turn them into repeat buyers."

Such findings are indicative of other studies that say the sales growth, although not continuing at such a major rise as today, will still bring in billions of dollars. In June 2008, the e-commerce research source eMarketer® published the following based on Department of Commerce statistics: U.S. retail e-commerce sales, except for travel, reached $146 billion in 2008, an increase of 14.3 percent over 2007, which totaled $127.7 billion. Other reports state that this increase will be even larger, and e-commerce in Europe is expected to be up 27 percent from 2007 to 2008.

From 2007 to 2012, sales in the U.S. will increase at an 11.3 percent average annual growth rate. In 2007, almost four-fifths of American Internet users, or 133 million individuals, shopped online. By 2012, an additional 25 million people will join them, raising the amount to 158 million, or nearly 83 percent of Internet users.

Amazon has separate international sites that allow about 25 countries worldwide to buy goods and services. Global sales need to be pursued by Amazon and its affiliates to maximize growth and expansion. In 2005, for example, Amazon entered China through an entity called **Joyo.com**®. In 2008, **Joyo.com** opened up a new operations center in Beijing. Although in the past, Chinese have placed an emphasis on saving and been reluctant to use credit or buy online, this is changing with the younger population. The China Market Research Group conducted interviews with 500 young adults between 18 and 32 years of age across China, and nearly 80 percent said they made an online purchase in the last six months. The vast majority expected to buy again in the next quarter. 70 percent said they would use a credit card for online purchases if they had one. They said as long as they trust the seller, they will buy items online. Surveys also show that more than eight out of ten Japanese and South Koreans used the Internet to buy items, and China is expected to surpass these numbers within a few years. In other words, the world is open to those individuals who have the determination and fortitude and decide to spend the needed time, energy, and resources to establish and grow an online business.

CASE STUDY: ANDY AND DEBBIE MOWERY

Andy and Debbie Mowery
Debnroo, Inc.
Ft. Collins, Colorado
970-416-6300
www.debnroo.com

CLASSIFIED CASE STUDIES
directly from the experts

Andy and Debbie Mowery, who own two Amazon stores for pet supplies, as well as another online business on their own for home and garden merchandise, made the move from eBay, where they were highly successful, to Amazon in 2007 to grow their business even more. Since then, they have had a "good, solid revenue stream" of income. "I wish I had taken this step even earlier," said Andy Mowery.

The Mowerys are examples of e-commerce entrepreneurs of the future who look at every angle possible for growth and presently see Amazon as the right avenue for their efforts. Not only are they Amazon Associates and WebStore owners, but they also are suppliers to Amazon for some of their pet items. In addition, they participate in "Clickriver," an Amazon pay-for-click program that allows advertisers to purchase sponsored links alongside Amazon products.

Andy Mowery calls Amazon "the best mousetrap to capture today's online buyers." He adds that yesterday was the time to jump onto Amazon. There are some categories that are already saturated and closed for new store owners, but that should not discourage anyone. "You need to be open to new ideas and realize there are many other ways to succeed." The goal should be, he said, "getting into Amazon any way that you can."

APPENDIX A

Glossary

An entirely new vocabulary has developed from the Internet in a little more than a decade. Before proceeding into the virtual world of online selling, it is important to become acquainted with these new terms.

Affiliate: A typical term for one Web site that drives traffic to another in exchange for a percent of sales from users attracted to the site. Amazon refers to its affiliates as "Associates."

Amazon item: Product Amazon sells and fulfills, not by a third-party merchant.

Amazon Qualifying Product: Product that Amazon has sold and fulfilled or that has been fulfilled for Amazon and is allowable to have a referral fee based on the operating agreement.

Analytics/Web Analytics: A tool that measures the impact of a Web site on its users. E-commerce organizations frequently rely on analytics software in order to create reports on measures including the how many were visitors, converted to buyers, or unique to the site; how they arrived at the Web site; which keywords were entered into the site's search engine; the length of time they stayed on a page or the entire site; the links that were clicked on; and when the visitors left the site.

Application Program (Application): Any program created to perform a specific function for the user, such as word processors, database programs, Web browsers, development tools, and drawing programs.

Associates Central: This Web site offers Amazon Associates numerous services, such as tools for creating reports and link-generation, a graphics reservoir, and ways to enhance online marketing.

Basic Display Product Link: Text descriptions of the products that link to pages with additional product information. They may be used by Amazon Associates to use as the item's text description and to send buyers to the product's offer listing page that consists of any new and used items available from individual sellers.

Blog: Comes from Weblog, or a journal that is available on the Web. To update a blog is "blogging," and a person who writes a blog is a "blogger." New blogs are normally written every day on a site created by software that is easy to use and maintain even without a great deal of technical knowhow.

Brick(s)-and-mortar: A business or a store with a physical, rather than a virtual, presence.

Browser: An application that offers users a way to search for and utilize the many different options on the Web. The term was first used with the Internet prior to the introduction of the World Wide Web as a user interface that allows visitors to navigate online and read the text files. Main browsers include Internet Explorer, Chrome, Safari, and Firefox.

B2C / Business-to-Consumer: In e-commerce, when a business is selling to individual consumers.

Button: A small, interactive graphic online that is normally used for advertising purposes. This is often a way for affiliates and sponsorships to drive traffic.

Category Targeting: Delivery of a specific message to categorized Web sites to reach users who are expected to find the products or services being offered of interest. It is a way to improve the effectiveness of a marketing campaign.

Click-through Rate (CTR): The rate users click on a product advertisement. To measure CTR, the total of times that users click on an ad is divided by how many times the ad is delivered.

Conversion: The percentage of how many products are shipped divided by how many clicks on a Web site link. If a Web site gets 200 clicks and those referrals generated 18 shipped items, the conversion rate would be 18/200=0.09, or 9 percent.

Cross-Selling: Offering similar merchandise to a customer who previously bought one product in order to encourage that person to make another similar purchase.

Daily Trends Report: Amazon displays the daily click and ordered items total and conversion, which allows Associates to immediately determine how well their site is doing.

Domain Name: The unique identification of a Web site. There are always two or more parts that are separated by dots.

Domain Name System (DNS): Converts Internet domain names into Internet protocol numbers. A DNS server performs this kind of translation.

E-commerce/Electronic Commerce: A structure used for establishing a business on the Web or for the online shopping industry.

E-mail: Electronic mail, normally in text form, that a person sends to another through the computer.

E-tailer: A company that sells items on the Web, just as traditional merchants do offline.

Extensible Markup Language (XML): Provides a standard way for developers to exchange information about sets of data and their organization.

Extensible Stylesheet Language Transformations (XSLT): A stylesheet language for XML.

Hard Drive Space: The main storage area in a computer that can maintain large amounts of data.

Hit: A request that is received from a Web browser for another item that comes from the Web server.

Homepage: Traditionally, this is the Web page that comes up first when the browser is started. Also, the user makes it the mainly used Web page.

Hyperlinks (Links): Hypertext connections among Web pages.

HyperText Markup Language (HTML): The coding language that gives information to the Web browser on the way to display a Web page's words and images.

Hypertext Transfer Protocol (HTTP): A set of rules for the transfer of files on the Internet. It also provides a standard for Web browsers and servers to communicate.

Impressions: Number of times that the links are viewed by users.

Internet: Networks that are interconnected using protocols. The Internet connects hundreds of thousands independent networks across the globe. The World Wide Web, or Web, provides a means of accessing information over the Internet.

Internet Protocol (IP): The method, or "protocol," utilized to transmit data among computers online. Each Internet computer, or host, has at least one uniquely identifying IP address that separates it from all other online computers.

Keyword: A word or group of words that focus a Web search and that targets marketing. Advertisers often buy keywords on search engines to promote their Web site content.

Link Type: The many ways that Amazon merchants have to link from their site to Amazon. These include:

Product Links: Connect to detail pages of individual Amazon products or by a third-party seller.

Recommended Products Links: Updated each time a Web page loads with new content that matches a chosen product category or keyword.

Search Box Links: Links in which users can enter search terms and get Amazon results.

Banner Links: Send customers directly to the Amazon homepage or product category, or feature a special marketing message.

Easy Links: Dynamically updated and homepage links.

Text Links: Any link redirecting visitors to specific Amazon pages, such as "Favorite Destinations" and "Link to Any Page."

Web Services Links: Individual product links that make SOAP and HTTP requests; add-to-cart buttons permitting users to add merchandise to their shopping carts; and remote-shopping-cart links giving visitors the opportunity to maintain a shopping cart on a site and then, when ready to check out, transfer to Amazon.

Link-Type Reports: Show performance of various Amazon links on a Web site with clicks, purchased items, shipped merchandise, conversion, and referrals.

Merchant Account: An Internet bank account that a site requires to receive electronic payments.

Meta Tag: "Meta" means "about this subject." This consists of information that a visitor does not see on the Web site, but rather is used to provide search engines with an easier way to categorize the contents of a page.

Navigation: This online feature allows users to move from one place to another by clicking on links in a menu bar.

1-Click (One Click): Amazon received a patent so that customers only have to enter their credit card number and address information on their first purchase. Each time they return to the Web site, they just click once to make a purchase and all their information is stored.

Online Store: A business-to-customer or business-to-business virtual e-commerce Web site that features and sells merchandise or services.

Orders Reports: Provides information on the items visitors have ordered on Amazon and the links that have been most effective. The figures are based on items ordered, but may not yet be shipped.

Password: A code provided that allows users to gain access to a private online area.

Pay-Per-Click: A means for driving traffic to a Web site using research engine advertising; it is necessary to pay only when someone visits the designated Web site.

Print-On-Demand (POD): Companies that self-published authors use to print books, DVDs, and CDs one at a time.

Product Link Clicks: This is the total amount of clicks

visitors have made on product links that are on the Amazon merchant Web site.

Product Link Conversion: This shows the frequency of Amazon visitors clicking on product links and then purchasing the item highlighted. To determine the conversion rate, one divides the sum of highlighted items purchased by the sum of product link clicks. The total is expressed in percentage form. For instance, if a visitor clicks on one of the Web site product links for a computer printer and then purchases it, the conversion for the product link is 100 percent. If another visitor clicks on the computer printer link but instead purchases a camera, the conversion rate falls to 50 percent (one item purchased/two direct-link clicks).

Random Access Memory (RAM): The most common computer memory that programs use to perform essential tasks when the computer is engaged.

Relevance Ranking: The measure of how effectively the indexed page responds to the search query when there are numerous matches to that question.

Really Simple Syndication (RSS): An XML-based vocabulary for distributing Web content allowing users to have new content delivered to a computer or mobile device as soon as published.

Search Engine: A means for searching for information on the Web, including such sites as Google, Bing, Yahoo!, and Ask.

Search Engine Marketing: An approach, often involving

paid ads, created to enhance the visibility of a Web site when conducting a search such as on Google.

Search Engine Optimization (SEO): The way to design Web pages so they get as high a ranking as possible in search engine results.

Seller: Whoever fulfills the order, whether it is Amazon or a third-party merchant.

Sellers Central: This is how merchants manage their WebStore, sell on Amazon, and interface with Fulfillment by Amazon. It provides them with an efficient and easy way to access the different areas of their Web site. With this support, the sellers can add or change product data, update inventory, get orders, and create their WebStore.

Shopping Cart/Shopping Basket: Online merchants use this software to help visitors add items to their cart after making a purchase. When they are ready to check out, the software adds the total price for the order, including shipping and handling.

Simple Object Access Protocol (SOAP): A simple XML-based protocol to allow applications to exchange information over HTTP.

Targeting: This is the use of advertisements that are designed to appeal to users who fit a particular marketing delineation.

Tracking: Online real-time reporting to measure the impact of advertisements on users.

Transaction: The act of purchasing a product or service from an e-commerce Web site.

Web Site Traffic: The number of visitors who view a Web site.

Uniform Resource Locator (URL): A Web page address. The beginning of the address is the protocol identifier, and the end specifies the IP address and the domain name.

Unique Visitors: In Web marketing, individuals who have gone to a Web site or obtained specific content, such as advertisements or e-mail, for a specified period of time such as a day or month.

Web Crawler: An electronic "robot" that connects to interacting computer systems and also compiles an index of links to documents.

Web Page: A document created to be viewed in a Web browser.

Web Site: The entire number of Web pages and other content, such as visuals, audio, and video files, which are located at the same Internet location.

World Wide Web (or Web): A network of interlinked hypertext documents accessed through the Internet.

 # BIBLIOGRAPHY

Bausch, Paul. *Amazon Hacks*. Sebastopol, CA: O'Reilly & Associates, 2003

Friedman, Mara. *Amazon.com for Dummies*. Hoboken, NJ: Wiley Publishing, 2004

Grey, Jim. "Conversation with Werner Vogels." **www.acmqueue.com/modules.php?name=Content&pa=show page&pid=388**

Hof, Robert D. *Business Week* "Amazon Wants to Run Your Business." November 13, 2006. **www.businessweek.com/ magazine/ content/06_46/b4009008.htm**

Holden, Greg. *Selling Beyond eBay*. New York: American Management Association, *2006 Journal of Advertising Research*. "The Relationship between Interactive Functions and Website" 44.4, Dec 2004

Machan, Dyan. "Jeff Bezos on the Future of Amazon.com." *Smart-Money*. November 28, 2008.

Nocera, Joe."Put Buyers First? What a Concept." *The New York Times*. January 5, 2008

Poynter, Dan. *Self-Publishing Manual*. Santa Barbara, CA: Para Publishing, 2006

Ravenscroft, Anthony. *Other People's Treasures*. Selling Books & CDs on Amazon.com. Santa Fe, NM, Fenris Brothers, 2005

Sampson, Brent. *Sell Your Book on Amazon*. Denver, CO: Outskirts Press, 2007

Seda, Catherine. *Search Engine Advertising*. Indianapolis, IN: New Riders, 2004

Sweeney, Susan. *101 Ways to Promote Your Web Site*. Gulf Breeze, FL:Maximum Press, 2005

Windwalker, Stephen. *Selling Used Books Online*. Belmont, MA: Harvard Perspectives Press, 2002

Zimmerman, Jan. *Web Marketing for Dummies*. Hoboken, NJ: Wiley Publishing, 2007

www.smartmoney.com/Investing/Stocks/Jeff-Bezos-on-the-Future-of-Amazon-com/

 **AUTHOR BIOGRAPHY**

During her years as a communication consultant for nonprofit and business clients, Sharon L. Cohen watched and appreciated the rise of the Internet as it impacted and changed the world, as it did in her own life. Once spending most of her time publishing print marketing and information materials and books for nonprofit organizations and corporations, she now communicates online to complete writing projects for businesses; offers grammatical and literary advice to students; interfaces with newfound associates and old friends worldwide; and finds answers to arcane research questions with several Google clicks. With a passion for writing and reading, she has spent many a day visiting and working in libraries, and perusing and ordering books from Amazon. She continues to watch with appreciation the way the Internet may be used to enhance world communication and shared learning, and bring education and literacy to the global village.

Cohen is also the author of *Yahoo! Income: How Anyone of Any Age, Location, and/or Background Can Build a Highly Profitable Online Business with Yahoo; 199 Internet-Based Businesses You Can Start with Less than One Thousand Dollars: Secrets, Techniques, and Strategies Ordinary People Use Every Day to Make Millions;* and *How to Open & Operate a Financially Successful Used Bookstore on Amazon and Other Web Sites: With Companion CD-ROM* (**www.atlantic-pub.com**).

 **INDEX**

A

Unique visitor count, 153-154

W

Whispernet, 221

Widgets, 24, 68, 177, 179-180,
182, 185, 188-190, 195-196, 199-
200, 203, 207-209, 231, 242, 252,
259, 291, 295, 309-310, 8